PRAGUE CZECH REPUBLIC TRAVEL GUIDE 2024 – 2025

The Ultimate Resource for Itineraries, Transportation,
Where to Stay, What to See, Where to Eat, and Insider Tips

Sandi H. Newman

Disclaimer
The information contained in this book is for general informational purposes only. While the author has made every effort to ensure the accuracy and completeness of the information provided, we make no representations or warranties of any kind, express or implied, about the accuracy, reliability, suitability, or availability with respect to the book or the information, products, services, or related graphics contained in the book for any purpose. Any reliance you place on such information is therefore strictly at your own risk.

The author will not be liable for any false, inaccurate, inappropriate, or incomplete information presented in this book. The author will not be liable for any damages of any kind arising from the use of this book, including but not limited to direct, indirect, incidental, punitive, and consequential damages.

The author does not assume and hereby disclaims any liability to any party for any loss, damage, or disruption caused by errors or omissions, whether such errors or omissions result from negligence, accident, or any other cause.

All information is provided "as is" with no guarantee of completeness, accuracy, timeliness, or of the results obtained from the use of this information, and without warranty of any kind, express or implied, including, but not limited to warranties of performance, merchantability, and fitness for a particular purpose.

This book includes links to other websites for informational purposes only. These links do not signify an endorsement of the content or opinions contained within those websites. The author has no control over the nature, content, and availability of those sites.

Travel information such as visa requirements, transportation schedules, prices, and business operations are subject to change and may vary. It is recommended that travelers verify such information independently.

Any product names, logos, brands, and other trademarks or images featured or referred to within this book are the property of their respective trademark holders. These trademark holders are not affiliated with the author, and they do not sponsor or endorse this book.

The author reserves the right to make changes or updates to the content of this book at any time without prior notice. By using this book, you agree to the terms of this disclaimer. If you do not agree with any part of this disclaimer, do not use this book.

pastry. There are also many international restaurants, so you can find something to suit every taste.

Prague is a great city for shopping. You can find everything from high-end fashion to unique souvenirs. Pařížská Street is known for its luxury boutiques, while the local markets are great for finding handmade items and local products.

Getting around Prague is easy. The city has an excellent public transportation system, including trams, buses, and the metro. You can also explore the city on foot or by bike. The streets of Prague are safe and easy to navigate.

When planning your trip to Prague, it is important to consider the best time to visit. The city has something to offer in every season. Spring and summer are great for enjoying the parks and gardens. In the fall, you can experience the beautiful autumn colors. Winter is magical, with Christmas markets and festive decorations.

Before you travel, make sure you have all the necessary documents. This includes your passport and any required visas. It is also a good idea to have travel insurance to cover any unexpected events. Packing the right items is important too. Prague has a temperate climate, so bring clothes that you can layer. Comfortable shoes are a must, as you will be doing a lot of walking.

This guide also includes practical tips to help you make the most of your trip. You will find information on how to avoid tourist traps, stay safe, and respect local customs. We have also included a section on useful Czech phrases to help you communicate with the locals.

Day trips from Prague are a great way to see more of the Czech Republic. You can visit the beautiful town of Český Krumlov, the stunning Karlštejn Castle, and the natural beauty of Bohemian Switzerland National Park. These trips are easy to organize and will add even more to your experience.

Prague is a city that captures the hearts of all who visit. It is a place where you can step back in time while enjoying all the comforts of a modern city. Whether you are interested in history, culture, food, or just exploring, Prague has something for you. This guide is designed to help you discover all the hidden gems, sightseeing wonders, and rich history that this incredible city has to offer.

We hope you find this guide helpful and that it inspires you to make the most of your time in Prague. Enjoy your journey through one of Europe's most enchanting cities.

TABLE OF CONTENTS

INTRODUCTION

This guide is your ticket to exploring one of the most beautiful cities in Europe. Prague is a city where history and modernity blend seamlessly. Whether you are a solo traveler, a couple, or a family, there is something here for everyone.

Prague is often called the "City of a Hundred Spires" because of its many churches and towers. As you walk through the city, you will see Gothic, Renaissance, and Baroque architecture at every turn. The Charles Bridge, with its statues and stunning views, is a must-see. The Old Town Square, with its famous Astronomical Clock, is another highlight. These are just a few examples of the many beautiful sights you will find in Prague.

But Prague is not just about its historical landmarks. It is also a vibrant, modern city with a rich cultural scene. There are many museums and galleries to explore, such as the National Museum and the DOX Centre for Contemporary Art. If you are interested in music, you can enjoy performances of classical music, jazz, and rock. Prague has a lively nightlife, with many bars, clubs, and live music venues to choose from.

One of the best things about Prague is its food. Czech cuisine is hearty and delicious. You can try traditional dishes like goulash, roast pork with dumplings, and trdelník, a sweet the famous Bone Church, or explore the stunning Karlštejn Castle. The Bohemian Switzerland National Park offers beautiful hiking trails and natural scenery. These trips are easy to organize and will add even more to your experience.

Visiting Prague is not just about seeing the sights; it is also about experiencing the local culture and way of life. The city has a relaxed and friendly atmosphere, and you will find that the locals are welcoming and helpful. Whether you are exploring the historic streets, enjoying a meal at a local restaurant, or shopping for souvenirs, you will feel like you are part of the city.

Prague is a city that offers a perfect blend of history, culture, and modernity. Its stunning architecture, rich history, vibrant arts scene, delicious food, and friendly atmosphere make it a must-visit destination. Whether you are a first-time visitor or a seasoned traveler, Prague has something to offer you. This guide will help you make the most of your trip and discover all the hidden gems, sightseeing wonders, and rich history that Prague has to offer. Enjoy your journey through one of Europe's most enchanting cities.

HOW TO USE THIS GUIDE

Welcome to your comprehensive travel guide to Prague and its enchanting surroundings! This guide has been meticulously crafted to ensure that your visit is as enjoyable and seamless as possible. Whether you are a first-time visitor or a seasoned traveler, this guide is designed to provide you with valuable insights, practical tips, and detailed information to make the most of your time in Prague. Here's how to navigate and use this guide effectively:

The guide is organized into clear, concise sections to help you find the information you need quickly and easily. Each chapter focuses on a specific aspect of your trip, from must-see landmarks and local dining spots to cultural etiquette and day trip suggestions. The detailed table of contents at the beginning of the book allows you to quickly locate the sections of interest.

Each section provides in-depth descriptions and useful tips. Whether it's the history of an iconic landmark, a recommended itinerary, or advice on avoiding tourist traps, every entry is designed to enrich your travel experience. Take your time to read through these descriptions to fully appreciate what Prague has to offer.

Throughout the guide, you will find practical tips highlighted for easy reference. These tips cover a wide range of topics, including transportation, dining, shopping, and safety. They are intended to provide you with useful advice that will help you navigate the city like a local.

Understanding the local culture can greatly enhance your travel experience. This guide includes sections on cultural etiquette, local customs, and traditions to help you connect more deeply with Prague and its people. Familiarize yourself with these insights to show respect and appreciation for the local culture.

To help you navigate Prague with ease, we have included a detailed map of the city. This map is accessible via a QR code for paperback readers and a clickable link for e-book readers.

For paperback readers:
1. Locate the QR code printed within this guide.
2. Open the camera app on your smartphone or QR code scanning app.
3. Point your camera at the QR code.
4. A notification or link will appear on your screen. Tap on it to open the map in your web browser.

For e-book readers:
1. Click on the clickable link provided just below the guide.
2. The link will open the map in your web browser.

The map provides a comprehensive overview of Prague, including major landmarks, transportation hubs, dining spots, and other points of interest. You can zoom in and out, search for specific locations, and plan your routes. Use the map to get a sense of the city's layout and to help you navigate from one place to another.

This guide is designed to be flexible and cater to different travel styles and preferences. Use the information provided to plan your itinerary based on your interests, time constraints, and budget.

We hope this guide serves as a valuable companion on your journey through Prague.

CHAPTER 1

GETTING TO KNOW PRAGUE

The History of Prague

Prague, the capital of the Czech Republic, has a rich and fascinating history that spans over a thousand years. This city has witnessed the rise and fall of empires, the flourishing of arts and culture, and significant political changes. Understanding the history of Prague helps to appreciate its beauty and cultural significance.

Prague's story begins in the 9th century when it was established as a fortified settlement on the banks of the Vltava River. The area where Prague now stands was originally inhabited by Celtic and Germanic tribes. The first major Slavic settlement appeared around the 6th century. By the late 9th century, the Přemyslid dynasty, a ruling family, began to build fortifications, including the Vyšehrad Castle and Prague Castle, making Prague a significant political and cultural center.

The city continued to grow in importance during the reign of King Wenceslas I in the 13th century. He invited German merchants and craftsmen to settle in Prague, which helped the city to flourish. This period saw the foundation of the Old Town and the construction of many significant buildings.

The establishment of the Old Town Square marked the heart of the city, where trade and social life thrived.

In the 14th century, under the rule of Emperor Charles IV, Prague reached its golden age. Charles IV made Prague the capital of the Holy Roman Empire and initiated many architectural and cultural projects. He founded Charles University in 1348, which is the oldest university in Central Europe. He also commissioned the construction of the Charles Bridge, connecting the Old Town with the Lesser Town. During this time, Prague became one of the largest and most prosperous cities in Europe.

However, Prague's fortunes fluctuated in the following centuries. The Hussite Wars in the early 15th century brought significant turmoil. These wars were sparked by religious reforms proposed by Jan Hus, a Czech priest who criticized the Catholic Church. After his execution in 1415, his followers, known as Hussites, revolted. The wars that followed led to considerable destruction in Prague and across Bohemia.

In the 16th century, Prague experienced a renaissance under the Habsburg rule. The city became a center of art and science, attracting scholars, artists, and alchemists. Emperor Rudolf II moved his court to Prague in 1583, bringing with him a period of cultural and scientific revival. The city's architecture saw the addition of many beautiful Renaissance and Baroque buildings.

The Thirty Years' War, which began in 1618, had a devastating impact on Prague. The conflict started with the famous Defenestration of Prague, where Protestant nobles threw Catholic officials out of a castle window. This event marked the beginning of a brutal war that ravaged much of Europe. Prague was occupied by various armies, and its population suffered greatly.

Despite these challenges, Prague continued to rebuild and grow. In the 18th and 19th centuries, the city saw a resurgence in cultural and intellectual life. The National Revival movement sought to restore Czech language and culture, which had been suppressed under Habsburg rule. This period saw the establishment of many cultural institutions, including the National Theatre and the National Museum.

The 20th century brought further changes and challenges to Prague. After World War I, Czechoslovakia was established as an independent country with Prague as its capital. The interwar period was a time of cultural and economic prosperity. However, World War II brought occupation and suffering. Prague was occupied by Nazi Germany from 1939 to 1945. Many of the city's Jewish residents were deported and perished in concentration camps.

After the war, Prague fell under Soviet influence and became the capital of communist Czechoslovakia. The Prague

Spring of 1968 was a significant event during this time. It was a period of political liberalization and reform led by Alexander Dubček. However, the movement was crushed by a Soviet-led invasion in August 1968.

The Velvet Revolution of 1989 marked the end of communist rule in Czechoslovakia. Peaceful protests led to the overthrow of the communist government, and Václav Havel, a playwright and dissident, became the country's president. In 1993, Czechoslovakia peacefully split into two countries: the Czech Republic and Slovakia, with Prague remaining the capital of the Czech Republic.

Today, Prague is a vibrant and modern city that honors its rich history. It is a place where you can see centuries-old buildings standing next to modern architecture. The city continues to be a center of culture, education, and politics. It attracts millions of visitors each year who come to experience its unique blend of history and contemporary life.

Prague's history is a needlepoint of triumphs and tragedies, of cultural flowering and political upheaval. Each era has left its mark on the city, creating a rich and complex heritage. As you walk through Prague, you are walking through centuries of history, where every street and building has a story to tell. This is what makes Prague not just a city, but a living museum, where the past is always present.

Geography and Climate

Prague, the capital city of the Czech Republic, is situated in the heart of Europe. Its unique geography and climate play a significant role in shaping the city's character and charm. Understanding the geography and climate of Prague helps to appreciate why this city has been a center of culture, politics, and tourism for centuries.

Prague is located in the central part of the Czech Republic, in the region known as Bohemia. The city lies on the Vltava River, which flows from the south to the north. The Vltava is the longest river in the Czech Republic, stretching over 430 kilometers. It divides Prague into two main parts, creating a natural beauty that adds to the city's picturesque landscape. The river has many bridges, with the most famous being the Charles Bridge, which connects the Old Town with the Lesser Town.

The city is built on a series of hills, which gives it a distinctive topography. There are nine major hills in Prague, including Letná, Vitkov, and Petřín. These hills provide stunning views of the city and are home to several parks and historical sites. Petřín Hill, for example, is a popular spot for both locals and tourists. It has a funicular railway that takes visitors to the top, where they can enjoy the Petřín Lookout Tower, a smaller version of the Eiffel Tower in Paris. The hill also has beautiful gardens and the famous Mirror Maze.

Prague's geographical location in central Europe means it has a temperate climate. The city experiences all four seasons, each bringing its own charm. The climate is characterized by mild summers, cold winters, and moderate rainfall throughout the year.

Spring in Prague, from March to May, is a beautiful time to visit. The weather starts to warm up, and the city comes to life with blooming flowers and green trees. The average temperatures range from 8°C in March to 18°C in May. Spring showers are common, so it's a good idea to bring an umbrella or a raincoat.

Summer, from June to August, is the warmest season in Prague. The average temperatures range from 15°C to 25°C, but it can occasionally reach up to 30°C during heatwaves. The long daylight hours provide ample time to explore the city's outdoor attractions. Summer is also the peak tourist season, so you can expect larger crowds at popular sites. The Vltava River becomes a hub of activity, with people enjoying boat rides and riverside picnics.

Autumn, from September to November, brings cooler temperatures and colorful foliage. The average temperatures range from 14°C in September to 6°C in November. This season is ideal for those who enjoy a quieter atmosphere, as the tourist crowds begin to thin out. The city's parks and gardens are particularly beautiful during this time, with leaves turning shades of red, orange, and yellow.

Winter in Prague, from December to February, is cold and often snowy. The average temperatures range from -1°C to 3°C. Snowfall is common, especially in January and February, transforming Prague into a winter wonderland. The city is known for its charming Christmas markets, which are set up in various squares, including the Old Town Square and Wenceslas Square. Visitors can enjoy hot mulled wine, traditional Czech snacks, and festive decorations.

Prague's climate is influenced by its geographical location between the oceanic climate of Western Europe and the continental climate of Eastern Europe. This results in relatively stable weather patterns, with no extreme temperatures or weather conditions. However, the weather can be unpredictable at times, so it's always a good idea to check the forecast and pack accordingly.

The geography and climate of Prague also play a role in the city's flora and fauna. The city is home to several parks and green spaces, such as Letná Park, Stromovka, and the Royal Garden at Prague Castle. These areas provide habitats for various plant and animal species, adding to the city's natural beauty. The Vltava River is home to fish species like trout, carp, and pike, and it's not uncommon to see swans and ducks swimming along the riverbanks.

In conclusion, the geography and climate of Prague contribute significantly to its appeal as a travel destination. The city's hills, river, and temperate climate create a picturesque and pleasant environment for residents and visitors alike. Whether you're exploring the historical sites, enjoying the parks and gardens, or simply taking in the views, Prague's unique geography and climate are sure to leave a lasting impression. This understanding of the city's natural features enhances the experience of visiting Prague and helps to appreciate the beauty and charm of this remarkable European capital.

Language, Currency, and Etiquette

Prague, the capital of the Czech Republic, is a city rich in culture and history. To fully appreciate and enjoy your time in Prague, it's important to understand the local language, currency, and etiquette. This knowledge will help you navigate the city more comfortably and interact with its residents respectfully.

The official language of Prague is Czech. Czech is a West Slavic language, closely related to Slovak and Polish. It has a rich linguistic history and is known for its complex grammar and pronunciation. While learning Czech might seem challenging, knowing a few basic phrases can greatly enhance your experience in Prague. Simple greetings such as "Dobrý den" (Good day) and "Děkuji" (Thank you) can go a long way in making a positive impression. Most people in Prague speak some English, especially those who work in tourism, restaurants, and shops. However, older generations might not be as fluent in English, so it's always helpful to know a few key Czech words and phrases. Signs and public information are often bilingual, with both Czech and English, which makes it easier for tourists to find their way around.

The currency used in Prague is the Czech koruna, abbreviated as CZK. While some places in Prague, especially in tourist areas, might accept euros, it's best to use the local currency to avoid any confusion or unfavorable exchange rates. The koruna is divided into 100 haléř, although coins in haléř are rarely used today. Banknotes come in denominations of 100, 200, 500, 1,000, 2,000, and 5,000 koruna, while coins come in 1, 2, 5, 10, 20, and 50 koruna. ATMs are widely available throughout the city, and credit cards are commonly accepted in most establishments. However, it's always a good idea to carry some cash, especially when visiting smaller shops, local markets, or using public transport. When exchanging money, it's advisable to use reputable exchange offices or banks to get the best rates and avoid any hidden fees.

Understanding local etiquette is crucial for showing respect and fitting in with the local culture. Czechs value politeness and formality, especially in public interactions. When greeting someone, it's customary to say "Dobrý den" (Good day) during the day and "Dobrý večer" (Good evening) in the evening. In more formal settings, titles are important. Use "Pan" (Mr.) and "Paní" (Mrs.) followed by the person's surname. Handshakes are the common form of greeting, and it's polite to make eye contact while shaking hands. When entering a shop or restaurant, it's customary to greet the staff with a simple "Dobrý den."

Dining etiquette in Prague also has its own set of rules. When dining out, wait to be seated by the host or hostess. Once seated, it's polite to say "Dobrou chuť" (Enjoy your meal) before starting to eat. When you're finished with your meal, place your knife and fork parallel on the plate to signal that you're done. Tipping is customary, and it's usual to leave around 10% of the bill as a tip. In some cases, rounding up the bill is also acceptable. It's polite to thank the staff as you leave, with a simple "Děkuji."

Public behavior in Prague is generally reserved. Loud talking or boisterous behavior in public places is frowned upon. On public transportation, it's expected to give up your seat to the elderly, pregnant women, or those with disabilities. When using escalators, stand on the right side to allow others to pass on the left. Queueing is also an important aspect of Czech etiquette; always wait your turn in lines and respect personal space.

Czechs take pride in their cultural heritage, and understanding this can enhance your visit. The country has a rich history in music, literature, and art. Attending a classical concert, visiting a museum, or exploring historical sites can provide deeper insights into Czech culture. When visiting religious sites or monuments, dress modestly and behave respectfully. Photography is often allowed, but it's polite to ask for permission if you're unsure.

When socializing with locals, be aware of certain cultural norms. Czechs appreciate punctuality, so it's important to be on time for appointments or social gatherings. When invited to someone's home, it's customary to bring a small gift, such as flowers or a bottle of wine. Avoid giving even numbers of flowers, as this is associated with funerals. During social interactions, Czechs may seem reserved at first, but once you get to know them, they can be very warm and hospitable.

Having a good grasp of the language, currency, and etiquette in Prague will make your visit more enjoyable and respectful. Knowing a few basic Czech phrases, using the local currency, and adhering to local customs will help you navigate the city with ease and make a positive impression on the locals. Prague is a city rich in culture and history, and understanding these aspects of daily life will allow you to fully appreciate and immerse yourself in all that this beautiful city has to offer.

CHAPTER 2

PLANNING YOUR TRIP

The Best Time to Visit Prague

The best time to visit Prague depends on what you want to experience during your trip. This beautiful city, with its rich history, stunning architecture, and vibrant culture, offers something unique in every season. Knowing the weather, tourist crowds, and local events throughout the year can help you decide when to plan your visit for the best experience.

Prague has a temperate climate, which means it experiences all four seasons. Each season has its own charm and provides different opportunities for exploration and enjoyment.

Spring, which lasts from March to May, is a delightful time to visit Prague. As the city shakes off the winter chill, the temperature gradually rises, ranging from 8°C in March to around 18°C in May. The blooming flowers and budding trees add a fresh and vibrant feel to the city's parks and gardens. This is a perfect time to explore outdoor attractions like the Petřín Hill, where you can enjoy the beautiful cherry blossoms and panoramic views of the city. The crowds are moderate, making it easier to visit popular sites like the Charles Bridge and Prague Castle without the summer rush. Spring also hosts several cultural events, including the

Prague Spring International Music Festival, which brings world-class performances to the city.

Summer, from June to August, is the warmest season in Prague. Temperatures typically range from 15°C to 25°C, although occasional heatwaves can push the mercury up to 30°C. The long daylight hours provide ample time for sightseeing and enjoying outdoor activities. Summer is also the peak tourist season, so you can expect larger crowds at major attractions. Despite this, the lively atmosphere and numerous outdoor events, such as open-air concerts and film screenings, make it an exciting time to visit. The Vltava River becomes a hub of activity, with boat tours and riverside picnics. If you enjoy warm weather and a bustling city vibe, summer is an excellent time to experience Prague.

Autumn, from September to November, brings cooler temperatures and a quieter atmosphere. The temperatures range from about 14°C in September to 6°C in November. The city's parks and gardens transform into a palette of red, orange, and yellow, creating picturesque scenery that is perfect for leisurely walks. Autumn is also harvest season, so you can enjoy local food festivals and markets offering fresh produce and traditional Czech delicacies. The tourist crowds start to thin out, allowing for a more relaxed exploration of the city's attractions. The St. Wenceslas Day celebrations in late September and the Signal Festival of lights in October are notable events that showcase Prague's cultural vibrancy during this season.

Winter, from December to February, is cold with average temperatures ranging from -1°C to 3°C. Snow is common, especially in January and February, transforming Prague into a winter wonderland. The city's Christmas markets are a major highlight, offering festive treats, handcrafted gifts, and a magical atmosphere. The markets in the Old Town Square and Wenceslas Square are particularly popular. Winter is also a great time to experience indoor attractions such as museums, galleries, and historic buildings without the summer crowds. If you enjoy winter sports, you can take a day trip to nearby ski resorts. Despite the cold, the cozy cafes and warm hospitality make winter a charming time to visit Prague.

When planning your trip, it's also worth considering the timing of major events and holidays. For instance, Easter in Prague is celebrated with colorful markets and traditional events. The city's Easter markets, much like the Christmas ones, offer a festive atmosphere with food, crafts, and performances. The Prague Fringe Festival in late May and early June brings a mix of theatre, comedy, and music, attracting artists and audiences from around the world.

In terms of accommodation and travel costs, the off-peak seasons of spring and autumn often provide better deals compared to the summer and winter holiday periods. If you're looking for a balance between favorable weather, manageable crowds, and reasonable prices, late spring and early autumn are ideal times to visit Prague.

The best time to visit Prague really depends on your preferences and what you wish to experience. Whether it's the blooming beauty of spring, the vibrant energy of summer, the colorful tranquility of autumn, or the festive charm of winter, Prague offers a unique and unforgettable experience in every season. By understanding the weather patterns, tourist dynamics, and seasonal events, you can plan a trip that aligns perfectly with your interests and expectations. This knowledge will ensure that your visit to Prague is as enjoyable and memorable as possible, allowing you to fully immerse yourself in the rich culture and history of this remarkable city.

Visa Requirements and Travel Documents for Visiting Prague

When planning a trip to Prague, one of the most important things to consider is the visa requirements and travel documents you will need. Ensuring that you have the correct paperwork will make your journey smooth and hassle-free. Understanding the process and requirements will help you prepare adequately for your visit to this beautiful city.

Prague is the capital of the Czech Republic, which is a member of the Schengen Area. The Schengen Area is a group of 27 European countries that have abolished border controls between each other, allowing for free and easy movement. If you are traveling to Prague, the type of visa you need will depend on your nationality and the purpose of your visit.

Citizens of the European Union (EU) and the European Economic Area (EEA) do not need a visa to enter the Czech Republic. They can travel to Prague with just a valid passport or national identity card. This ease of travel is one of the benefits of the EU and EEA agreements.

For citizens of many other countries, including the United States, Canada, Australia, and Japan, no visa is required for short stays of up to 90 days within a 180-day period. This visa-free access is for tourism, business trips, or family visits. However, even if you do not need a visa, you must still have a valid passport. Your passport should be valid for at least three months beyond your intended departure date from the Schengen Area and must have been issued within the last ten years.

If you are from a country that requires a visa to enter the Schengen Area, you will need to apply for a Schengen visa before your trip. The Schengen visa allows you to stay in the Schengen Area for up to 90 days within a 180-day period for tourism, business, or visiting family and friends. To apply for a Schengen visa, you will need to submit your application to the embassy or consulate of the Czech Republic or the country that is your main destination within the Schengen Area.

The process of obtaining a Schengen visa involves several steps. First, you need to fill out a visa application form. This form can usually be found on the website of the Czech embassy or consulate in your country. You will need to provide personal information, travel details, and the purpose of your visit.

Along with the application form, you will need to submit several supporting documents. These typically include:

1. A valid passport: Your passport must have at least two blank pages for the visa sticker and be valid for at least three months beyond your intended stay in the Schengen Area.

2. Passport-sized photographs: You will need to provide recent photos that meet the specific requirements for visa applications.

3. Travel itinerary: This includes your flight reservations, hotel bookings, and a detailed plan of your activities in Prague.

4. Proof of accommodation: You need to show where you will be staying during your visit, such as hotel reservations or an invitation letter from a host if you are staying with friends or family.

5. Travel insurance: You must have travel insurance that covers medical expenses and emergencies for the entire duration of your stay in the Schengen Area. The insurance should cover at least €30,000.

6. Proof of financial means: You need to demonstrate that you have sufficient funds to support yourself during your

stay. This can be shown through bank statements, a letter from your employer, or proof of income.

7. A cover letter: This letter should explain the purpose of your visit, your travel plans, and any other relevant information.

8. Visa fee: There is a fee for processing the Schengen visa application, which is usually paid at the time of submission.

Once you have gathered all the necessary documents, you will need to schedule an appointment at the Czech embassy or consulate. During the appointment, you will submit your application, provide your biometric data (fingerprints and a photograph), and possibly attend an interview.

The processing time for a Schengen visa can vary, but it generally takes about 15 days. It is recommended to apply for the visa well in advance of your planned trip to allow for any delays.

For longer stays or other purposes, such as studying, working, or joining family members, you may need a different type of visa or residence permit. These visas have additional requirements and longer processing times. It is important to check the specific requirements for your situation on the website of the Czech embassy or consulate.

In addition to visa requirements, there are other important travel documents to consider. Always carry a copy of your travel insurance policy, as well as emergency contact information. It is also a good idea to have copies of your passport and visa in case the originals are lost or stolen. Keep these copies in a separate place from the originals.

When traveling to Prague, it is also important to respect the immigration laws and regulations of the Czech Republic. Ensure that you do not overstay your visa or the permitted 90-day period if you are traveling visa-free. Overstaying can result in fines, deportation, and future travel restrictions to the Schengen Area.

Knowing the visa requirements and travel documents needed for visiting Prague is crucial for a smooth and enjoyable trip. Whether you need a visa or can travel visa-free, being well-prepared with the correct documentation will help you avoid any complications. By following the guidelines and ensuring that you have all the necessary paperwork, you can focus on enjoying your visit to this beautiful and historic city.

Health and Safety Tips

When visiting Prague, it is important to be aware of health and safety tips to ensure a smooth and enjoyable trip.

Firstly, it is important to understand the healthcare system in Prague. The city has a well-developed healthcare infrastructure, with many hospitals, clinics, and pharmacies available. If you need medical assistance, you can visit one of the hospitals, such as the General University Hospital or the Motol University Hospital. These hospitals have English-speaking staff and provide high-quality medical care. Pharmacies are widely available throughout the city, and many pharmacists speak English. They can provide over-the-counter medications for minor ailments, such as headaches or colds.

Before traveling to Prague, it is advisable to have travel insurance that covers medical expenses. This insurance should include coverage for emergencies, hospital stays, and medical evacuation if necessary. Carry a copy of your insurance policy with you, along with the contact information for your insurance provider. In case of a medical emergency, having this information readily available will help ensure you receive the necessary care.

It is also a good idea to bring a basic first aid kit with you, containing items such as band-aids, antiseptic wipes, pain relievers, and any prescription medications you may need. This kit can be useful for treating minor injuries or illnesses while traveling. If you have any specific health conditions or allergies, carry a medical alert card that provides information about your condition in both English and Czech. This card can be helpful in emergencies when communicating with medical personnel.

When it comes to food and water safety, Prague is generally safe. The tap water is safe to drink, and the city's restaurants and cafes maintain high hygiene standards. However, it is always a good idea to practice basic food safety measures. Avoid eating food that looks undercooked or has been left out for a long time. Wash your hands regularly, especially before eating. If you have a sensitive stomach, you may prefer to drink bottled water or use a water filter.

Prague is known for its beautiful architecture and historic sites, many of which involve walking and climbing stairs. Wearing comfortable shoes is essential, as you will likely be doing a lot of walking on cobblestone streets and uneven surfaces. Be mindful of your surroundings, especially in crowded areas, to avoid tripping or falling. If you plan to visit sites like Prague Castle or Petrin Hill, be prepared for some physical exertion. Pace yourself and take breaks if needed.

Public transportation in Prague is safe and reliable. The city has an extensive network of trams, buses, and metro lines that can take you to most tourist attractions. When using public transportation, keep an eye on your belongings to prevent pickpocketing. Pickpocketing can occur in crowded areas, such as trams or metro stations. Use a secure bag or money belt to keep your valuables safe. Be aware of your surroundings and avoid displaying expensive items, such as jewelry or electronics, in public.

Prague is generally a safe city, but it is always wise to take precautions to protect yourself and your belongings. Avoid walking alone in poorly lit areas at night, and stick to well-populated streets. If you need directions or assistance, seek help from official sources, such as police officers or staff at your hotel. Be cautious of strangers offering unsolicited help or trying to sell you something on the street.

Another important aspect of staying safe in Prague is understanding the local laws and customs. Respect local regulations and be aware of cultural norms. For example, it is illegal to drink alcohol in certain public places, and there are designated areas for smoking. Familiarize yourself with these rules to avoid any issues during your trip. Additionally, while Prague is a popular destination for its nightlife, always drink responsibly and be aware of your surroundings. If you plan to enjoy the city's bars and clubs, never leave your drink unattended and avoid accepting drinks from strangers.

Weather conditions can also affect your safety and comfort while visiting Prague. The city experiences all four seasons, each with its own weather patterns. In the winter, temperatures can drop below freezing, and snow is common. Dress in warm layers, wear a hat and gloves, and use non-slip footwear to navigate icy sidewalks. In the summer, temperatures can rise, so wear light clothing, use sunscreen, and stay hydrated. Check the weather forecast before heading out each day and dress appropriately for the conditions.

In case of an emergency, it is important to know the local emergency numbers. The general emergency number in the

Czech Republic is 112, which can be dialed for police, fire, or medical emergencies. Additionally, the number for medical emergencies is 155, and for the fire department, it is 150. Keep these numbers handy, and if you have a mobile phone, save them in your contacts for quick access.

Lastly, consider registering with your embassy or consulate when you arrive in Prague. This registration can provide you with important information and assistance in case of an emergency, such as a natural disaster or political unrest. The embassy can also help you with lost or stolen passports and other travel-related issues.

Being aware of health and safety tips can greatly enhance your experience while visiting Prague. By understanding the healthcare system, practicing food and water safety, taking precautions with public transportation, respecting local laws and customs, and being prepared for weather conditions, you can ensure a safe and enjoyable trip. Carry travel insurance, a first aid kit, and important contact information to be well-prepared for any situation. With these tips in mind, you can focus on exploring and enjoying all that Prague has to offer, knowing that you are taking the necessary steps to protect your health and safety.

Packing Essentials for a trip to Prague

Planning a trip to Prague involves more than just booking flights and accommodations. To make the most of your visit to this enchanting city, it's essential to prepare adequately and bring everything you might need.

Firstly, having the right travel documents is crucial. Make sure your passport is valid for at least three months beyond your planned departure from the Czech Republic. Depending on your nationality, you may also need a visa. For citizens of many countries, including those in the EU, the US, Canada, and Australia, a visa is not required for stays of up to 90 days. However, it's always best to check the latest requirements before you travel. Keep a copy of your passport and visa (if applicable) in a separate location from the originals in case they are lost or stolen. Having digital copies saved on your phone or email can also be helpful.

Travel insurance is another essential. Ensure your insurance covers medical emergencies, trip cancellations, and theft or loss of personal items. Carry a copy of your insurance policy and emergency contact numbers. If you require any prescription medications, bring enough to last your entire trip along with a copy of the prescription. It's also a good idea to carry a basic first aid kit with items like band-aids, antiseptic wipes, pain relievers, and any personal medications you might need.

When it comes to clothing, pack according to the season in which you will be visiting. Prague experiences all four seasons, each with distinct weather patterns. For winter, pack warm clothing such as thermal layers, a heavy coat, gloves, a hat, and a scarf, as temperatures can drop below freezing and snow is common. In spring and autumn, layers are key, as the weather can be quite variable. Include a mix of long-sleeved shirts, sweaters, and a light to medium-weight jacket. Summer in Prague can be warm, so bring light, breathable clothing like t-shirts, shorts, and dresses, as well as a hat and sunglasses. Comfortable walking shoes are a must, as Prague's cobblestone streets can be challenging to navigate in less supportive footwear. If you plan to dine in nicer restaurants or attend events like the opera, include a set of dressier clothes.

Prague has a reliable public transportation system, including trams, buses, and the metro. To use these services, you'll need to purchase tickets, which can be bought at ticket machines, newsstands, or via a mobile app. Consider buying a travel pass if you plan to use public transport frequently, as it can be more economical. Download maps and public transportation apps to your smartphone to help you navigate the city efficiently.

Electricity in the Czech Republic is 230 volts with a frequency of 50 Hz, and the power plugs and sockets are of type E. If your devices use a different type of plug or voltage, you'll need an appropriate adapter and possibly a voltage converter. Bring a universal adapter to ensure you can charge your electronics without any issues.

Staying connected while traveling is important. Although many hotels and cafes in Prague offer free Wi-Fi, consider purchasing a local SIM card or an international roaming plan for your mobile phone. This will help you stay connected for navigation, making reservations, or in case of emergencies. Ensure your phone is unlocked if you plan to use a local SIM card.

Packing some essential travel accessories can make your trip more comfortable. A good quality travel pillow, earplugs, and an eye mask can be invaluable for long flights or train journeys. A reusable water bottle is also handy, as tap water in Prague is safe to drink. A small daypack or crossbody bag is useful for carrying your daily essentials like your wallet, phone, camera, and guidebook.

When it comes to money, the currency used in Prague is the Czech koruna (CZK). It's a good idea to have some local currency on hand for small purchases, tips, and places that might not accept credit cards. ATMs are widely available, and credit cards are accepted in most establishments. However, be aware of potential foreign transaction fees from your bank. Inform your bank of your travel plans to avoid any issues with your cards. It's also wise to have a money belt or a secure wallet to keep your cash and cards safe, especially in crowded tourist areas where pickpocketing can occur.

Understanding a few basic Czech phrases can enhance your experience and help you connect with the locals. While many people in Prague speak English, particularly in tourist areas, knowing simple words like "Dobrý den" (Good day), "Prosím" (Please), and "Děkuji" (Thank you) is appreciated and can make interactions smoother. Consider carrying a small phrasebook or downloading a translation app to assist with language barriers.

Prague is rich in history and culture, so having a guidebook or downloading an app with information about the city's attractions can be very useful. This can provide context and enhance your understanding of the sites you visit, such as Prague Castle, Charles Bridge, and the Old Town Square. Researching in advance and planning an itinerary can help you make the most of your time and ensure you don't miss out on must-see attractions.

It's also important to consider your personal safety. Although Prague is generally safe, it's always wise to be vigilant. Keep an eye on your belongings in crowded places, avoid carrying large amounts of cash, and be cautious when withdrawing money from ATMs. If you're going out at night, stay in well-lit, populated areas, and avoid walking alone in unfamiliar places.

Finally, familiarize yourself with local customs and etiquette. The Czech people value politeness and respect. When greeting someone, a simple handshake and eye contact are appropriate. Tipping in restaurants is customary, usually around 10% of the bill if the service was satisfactory. When visiting religious sites or historical monuments, dress modestly and behave respectfully.

Being well-prepared for your trip to Prague involves more than just packing your bags. Ensuring you have the necessary travel documents, appropriate clothing, health and safety items, and a good understanding of local customs will help you have a smooth and enjoyable visit. With the right preparation, you can fully immerse yourself in the rich culture and history of this beautiful city, creating lasting memories of your time in Prague.

CHAPTER 3

GETTING THERE AND AROUND

Arriving in Prague

When planning a trip to Prague, it is essential to understand the various routes and modes of transportation available for arriving in the city. Prague is well-connected to many parts of the world, making it accessible by air, rail, road, and even by river.

Most international travelers arrive in Prague by air. The city's main airport is Václav Havel Airport Prague, located about 17 kilometers northwest of the city center. This modern airport handles flights from numerous international destinations, including major cities in Europe, Asia, and North America. Airlines such as Czech Airlines, British Airways, Lufthansa, and Emirates operate regular flights to and from Prague. Upon arrival at the airport, you have several options for reaching the city center. Taxis and ride-sharing services like Uber are available outside the terminal. Alternatively, the Airport Express bus provides a direct connection to the main train station (Praha hlavní nádraží), while public buses and metro services offer more economical options.

For those traveling from neighboring countries or other parts of Europe, arriving in Prague by train is a popular and scenic option. Prague is a major railway hub with connections to many European cities. The main train station, Praha hlavní nádraží, is located in the city center and is well-served by international and domestic trains. High-speed trains such as the EuroCity (EC) and InterCity (IC) connect Prague with cities like Berlin, Vienna, Budapest, and Munich. These trains are comfortable and offer amenities such as dining cars and Wi-Fi. Traveling by train allows you to enjoy the picturesque landscapes of Central Europe while avoiding the hassle of airport security and long check-in times.

Traveling to Prague by bus is another viable option, especially for those on a budget. The city is served by several international bus companies, including FlixBus, Eurolines, and RegioJet. These buses connect Prague with numerous cities across Europe, often at lower prices than train or air travel. The main bus station in Prague is Florenc, located near the city center and well-connected by public transportation. Long-distance buses are usually equipped with comfortable seats, Wi-Fi, and onboard restrooms, making the journey pleasant and convenient.

If you prefer to drive, arriving in Prague by car is also possible. The city is connected to major European highways, making it easily accessible from surrounding countries. The D1 motorway links Prague with Brno and Vienna, while the D5 connects the city with Plzeň and Germany. Driving to

Prague allows for flexibility and the opportunity to explore the countryside at your own pace. However, be aware of the parking regulations and traffic conditions in the city. Parking can be challenging in the city center, and it is often easier to use public transportation once you arrive.

For those who enjoy a leisurely and unique travel experience, arriving in Prague by river cruise is an option worth considering. The Vltava River, which runs through the heart of Prague, is part of the larger Elbe River system. Several river cruise companies offer journeys that include Prague as a stop or final destination. These cruises typically travel through Germany and the Czech Republic, offering a relaxing way to see the countryside and historic towns along the way. Upon arrival in Prague, the cruise ships dock near the city center, providing easy access to the main attractions.

Prague is a well-connected city with multiple routes and modes of transportation available for travelers. Whether you choose to arrive by air, train, bus, car, or river cruise, each option offers its own advantages and unique experiences. By understanding these different routes, you can plan your journey to Prague with confidence, ensuring a smooth and enjoyable start to your trip.

Map

Scan the QR code below to be redirected to the map of Prague (for paperback readers)

Click here to be redirected to the map of Prague for e-book readers.

Getting Around Prague

Public Transportation: Trams, Buses, and Metro

Getting around Prague is convenient and efficient, thanks to its well-developed public transportation system. The city is served by trams, buses, and a metro network, all of which are operated by the Prague Public Transit Company (DPP). Understanding how to use these modes of transport will make your visit to Prague much easier and more enjoyable.

The tram system in Prague is one of the most extensive and efficient in the world. Trams are a popular mode of transportation for both locals and tourists because they are reliable and cover a large part of the city. There are 25 daytime tram lines and 9 night tram lines, ensuring that you can get around at almost any hour. The trams are numbered and the routes are well-marked with maps and schedules at each stop. Trams generally run from 4:30 AM until midnight, with night trams operating on reduced schedules during the early hours. The frequency of trams varies depending on the time of day and the line, but they usually arrive every 4-10 minutes during peak hours. Riding a tram in Prague is also a scenic way to see the city, as many routes pass by major attractions and picturesque neighborhoods.

The Prague metro is another key component of the city's public transportation system. The metro network consists of three lines: A (green), B (yellow), and C (red). These lines intersect at central transfer stations, making it easy to switch lines and reach your destination. The metro operates from 5:00 AM to midnight, with trains running every 2-3 minutes during peak times and every 5-10 minutes during off-peak hours. The metro is known for its speed and efficiency, making it a preferred choice for longer distances and for getting to places quickly. The stations are equipped with clear signage in both Czech and English, which helps non-Czech speakers navigate the system with ease.

Buses in Prague complement the tram and metro networks by serving areas that are not easily accessible by other forms of public transport. There are both daytime and night bus services, with daytime buses operating from around 4:30 AM to midnight, and night buses running throughout the night. Buses are especially useful for reaching suburban areas and the outskirts of the city. The bus stops are marked with signs displaying the routes and schedules. Just like trams and the metro, buses in Prague are punctual and reliable.

To use the public transportation system in Prague, you need to purchase a ticket. Tickets are valid on trams, buses, and the metro, and can be bought at ticket machines located in metro stations, tram stops, and some bus stops. They are also available at newsstands, convenience stores, and via mobile apps. There are different types of tickets depending on the duration of your journey. The most common are the 30-minute and 90-minute tickets, but you can also purchase 24-

hour, 72-hour, and monthly passes if you plan to use public transportation frequently. It's important to validate your ticket in the yellow validation machines found on trams and buses, or at the entrance to metro stations, before starting your journey. Failure to do so can result in a fine if you are checked by an inspector.

The public transportation system in Prague is integrated, which means you can use the same ticket for all modes of transport. This integration makes it easy to switch between trams, buses, and the metro without needing to purchase multiple tickets. The network is designed to be user-friendly, with clear maps and signs to guide you. Additionally, most public transport vehicles are equipped with digital displays and audio announcements that indicate the next stop, making it easy to know where to get off.

Accessibility is also a priority in Prague's public transportation system. Many tram and metro stations are equipped with elevators and ramps to accommodate passengers with mobility issues. Some trams and buses have low-floor designs, making it easier to board and disembark. The public transportation company also provides detailed information about accessible routes and services on their website.

For tourists, the Prague Card is a convenient option. This card offers unlimited travel on public transportation for a set number of days, along with free or discounted entry to many of Prague's attractions. It can be purchased online or at various points in the city, including the airport, major metro stations, and tourist information centers.

Safety is an important aspect of Prague's public transportation. The system is generally very safe, with low levels of crime. However, it is always wise to stay aware of your surroundings and keep an eye on your belongings, especially in crowded areas. Pickpocketing can occur, as in any major city, so keeping your valuables secure is recommended.

The public transportation system in Prague, comprising trams, buses, and the metro, is a highly efficient and reliable way to navigate the city. The extensive network covers all major areas and attractions, making it easy for both locals and visitors to get around. By understanding how to use these services and where to purchase tickets, you can travel around Prague with confidence and ease. Whether you are commuting from one neighborhood to another or exploring the historical sites, Prague's public transport ensures you can do so conveniently and comfortably.

Taxis and Ride-Sharing Services

Getting around Prague using taxis and ride-sharing services can be a convenient and efficient way to navigate the city, especially if you prefer direct transportation or need to travel with luggage. Understanding how these services operate, what to expect, and how to ensure a smooth experience is essential for any visitor.

Taxis in Prague are readily available and can be hailed on the street, found at designated taxi stands, or booked via phone or app. The official taxis are generally reliable, but it's important to use reputable companies to avoid potential issues such as overcharging. Some of the well-known taxi companies in Prague include AAA Radiotaxi, City Taxi, and ProfiTaxi. These companies offer 24/7 service and have English-speaking operators, making it easier for tourists to arrange rides.

When hailing a taxi on the street, it's crucial to ensure that it is a legitimate, licensed taxi. Licensed taxis in Prague are usually yellow or white and display a "TAXI" sign on the roof. The side doors should have the company name, license number, and a fare chart indicating the rates. The base fare, per-kilometer rate, and waiting charge should be clearly visible. It is recommended to avoid unmarked taxis or those without proper identification, as these could be operated by unscrupulous drivers looking to overcharge tourists.

To avoid misunderstandings or disputes, always confirm the approximate fare with the driver before starting your journey. In Prague, the base fare is typically around 40 CZK, with an additional charge per kilometer, usually around 28 CZK, and a waiting fee per minute. While most taxi drivers are honest, confirming the fare can prevent any unpleasant surprises at the end of your ride. Additionally, make sure the taxi meter is turned on and working correctly throughout the journey.

For those who prefer a more modern approach, ride-sharing services like Uber and Bolt are widely used in Prague. These services offer a convenient and often more affordable alternative to traditional taxis. To use ride-sharing services, you will need to download the respective app on your smartphone, create an account, and link a payment method. Once you have done this, you can book a ride by entering your destination, and the app will provide an estimated fare and the driver's details.

One of the main advantages of using ride-sharing services is the ability to track your ride in real-time. The app shows the driver's location, estimated arrival time, and the route to your destination. This transparency adds a layer of safety and convenience, especially for those unfamiliar with the city. Furthermore, ride-sharing apps allow you to rate your driver and provide feedback, which helps maintain high service standards.

When using Uber or Bolt, you can choose from different types of rides, depending on your needs and budget. Options range from standard cars to larger vehicles for groups or luxury options for a more comfortable ride. The fare is calculated based on the distance and time of the journey, and payment is processed automatically through the app, eliminating the need to handle cash. This cashless system is particularly convenient for tourists who may not have local currency readily available.

While ride-sharing services are generally reliable, it's always good to follow some basic safety tips. Verify the driver and vehicle details provided in the app before getting into the car. Ensure the license plate, car model, and driver's photo match what is shown in the app. If you feel uncomfortable at any point, do not hesitate to cancel the ride and book another one. Sharing your trip details with a friend or family member via the app is also a good practice for added security.

Taxis and ride-sharing services are especially useful for getting to and from Prague's Václav Havel Airport, as they offer a direct and hassle-free mode of transportation. The airport is about 17 kilometers from the city center, and a taxi or ride-share can get you there in approximately 30 minutes, depending on traffic. While public transportation is available, a taxi or ride-share can be more convenient if you have a lot of luggage or if you arrive late at night.

It's also worth noting that Prague's city center can become quite congested, especially during peak hours. In such cases, using a taxi or ride-sharing service might take longer than anticipated. For shorter trips within the city center, walking or using public transportation such as trams or the metro might be faster and more efficient. However, for longer distances or when traveling to less accessible areas, taxis and ride-sharing services remain a convenient option.

Getting around Prague using taxis and ride-sharing services offers a flexible and convenient way to explore the city. By choosing reputable taxi companies or using trusted ride-sharing apps like Uber and Bolt, you can ensure a safe and comfortable journey. Understanding the fare structure, confirming the fare with the driver, and following basic safety tips will help you avoid any issues. Whether you're heading to the airport, exploring the city, or traveling with luggage, these services provide an efficient means of transportation, complementing Prague's extensive public transit network.

Renting a Car and Driving Tips

Renting a car and driving in Prague can be a convenient and flexible way to explore not only the city but also the beautiful countryside and nearby attractions. However, it requires some preparation and understanding of local driving rules and conditions.

When considering renting a car in Prague, the first step is to choose a reputable car rental company. International brands like Hertz, Avis, Budget, and Europcar, as well as local companies such as Czechocar and Rent Plus, operate in Prague. It's advisable to book your rental car in advance, especially during peak tourist seasons, to ensure availability and get the best rates. You can make reservations online through the rental company's website or through third-party booking platforms that compare prices and options.

To rent a car in Prague, you need to meet certain requirements. Most rental companies require drivers to be at least 21 years old, although some may have a higher minimum age requirement. Additionally, you must have held a valid driver's license for at least one year. If your driver's license is not in Roman script (for example, if it's in Cyrillic or Chinese characters), you will also need an International Driving Permit (IDP). Make sure to carry your passport and a credit card, as these are typically required for the rental agreement and deposit.

When picking up your rental car, inspect it carefully for any existing damage and make sure it is documented in the rental agreement to avoid any disputes when returning the vehicle. Familiarize yourself with the car's features and ensure you know how to operate the lights, windshield wipers, and other essential controls. If you are not accustomed to driving manual transmission vehicles, it's important to request an automatic car in advance, as manual transmission is more common in Europe.

Driving in Prague requires an understanding of local traffic rules and regulations. In the Czech Republic, you drive on the right-hand side of the road, and overtaking is done on the left. Seat belts are mandatory for all passengers, and using a mobile phone while driving is prohibited unless you have a hands-free system. The legal blood alcohol limit is 0.0%, meaning there is zero tolerance for drinking and driving.

Speed limits in the Czech Republic vary depending on the type of road and area. In urban areas, the speed limit is generally 50 km/h (31 mph). On rural roads, it is 90 km/h (56 mph), and on highways, the speed limit is 130 km/h (81 mph). Speed cameras and police patrols are common, so it is important to adhere to these limits to avoid fines.

Parking in Prague can be challenging, especially in the city center. There are different parking zones, each with its own rules and fees. Blue zones are reserved for residents, and parking in these areas requires a permit. Orange and green zones are for short-term parking, with orange zones allowing parking for up to two hours and green zones for up to six hours. You can pay for parking using ticket machines located nearby, which accept coins and sometimes credit cards. Always display the ticket on your dashboard. There are also parking garages and park-and-ride facilities on the outskirts of the city, which provide a more convenient option if you plan to spend the day exploring Prague on foot.

When driving in Prague, it's important to be aware of pedestrians, cyclists, and trams. Pedestrians have the right of way at marked crosswalks, and it is mandatory to stop for them. Cyclists often share the road with vehicles, so be cautious and give them plenty of space when overtaking. Trams are a common sight in Prague and have the right of way. Be particularly careful when crossing tram tracks, and never overtake a tram that has stopped to let passengers on or off.

Navigation can be a challenge if you are not familiar with the city. Using a GPS or a navigation app like Google Maps can help you find your way and avoid getting lost. Many rental cars come equipped with built-in GPS, but you can also use your smartphone. Make sure you have a mobile data plan or download offline maps before your trip.

Fuel stations are plentiful in Prague and the surrounding areas. Most stations accept credit cards, but it's a good idea to carry some cash as a backup. Fuel prices are displayed in liters, and you typically have the option of filling up with diesel or unleaded petrol. Pay attention to the type of fuel your rental car requires, as using the wrong type can cause significant damage.

Exploring Prague by car offers the flexibility to visit nearby attractions that may be difficult to reach by public transportation. Popular day trips include the medieval town of Český Krumlov, the spa town of Karlovy Vary, and the stunning Bohemian Switzerland National Park. Having a car allows you to set your own schedule and enjoy the scenic routes at your own pace.

Renting a car and driving in Prague can be a rewarding experience that provides freedom and convenience. By choosing a reputable rental company, understanding the local driving rules, and being prepared for the challenges of urban driving, you can ensure a safe and enjoyable journey. Whether you're exploring the city or venturing out to the beautiful Czech countryside, having a car gives you the flexibility to make the most of your visit.

Walking and Biking in Prague
Exploring Prague on foot or by bike is one of the best ways to truly experience the charm and beauty of this historic city. Walking and biking allow you to immerse yourself in the local culture, see hidden gems, and enjoy the city at a leisurely pace. This detailed explanation will provide you with everything you need to know about getting around Prague by walking and biking.

Prague is a city made for walking. Its compact layout, pedestrian-friendly streets, and beautiful architecture make it an ideal place to explore on foot. Many of the city's most famous attractions are located within walking distance of each other. For instance, you can easily walk from the Old Town Square to the Charles Bridge and then on to Prague Castle. Walking allows you to take in the intricate details of the city's Gothic, Baroque, and Renaissance buildings, as well as discover quaint cafes, shops, and hidden courtyards.

When walking in Prague, it's important to wear comfortable shoes. The city's historic center is paved with cobblestones, which can be hard on your feet if you're not prepared.

Additionally, Prague is built on a series of hills, so be ready for some uphill walking, especially if you're heading to places like Prague Castle or Petrin Hill. Take your time and enjoy the journey; there's no need to rush when you're surrounded by such beauty.

Prague's major streets and squares are well-marked with signs in both Czech and English, making it easy to find your way around. Tourist maps are available at hotels and information centers, and they can be very helpful in navigating the city. Many of the key landmarks and neighborhoods, such as the Old Town, Lesser Town, and New Town, are easily accessible on foot.

Walking tours are a popular way to explore Prague. These tours are led by knowledgeable guides who can provide historical context and interesting stories about the places you visit. There are various types of walking tours available, including general city tours, specialized tours focusing on specific themes like architecture or history, and even ghost tours. Joining a walking tour can enrich your experience and help you see the city from a local's perspective.

For those who prefer a more active mode of transportation, biking in Prague is a fantastic option. The city has become increasingly bike-friendly over the past few years, with new bike lanes and paths being added regularly. While Prague's hilly terrain can be challenging, especially for beginners, there are plenty of flat routes that are perfect for a leisurely ride.

To rent a bike in Prague, you can choose from several bike rental shops located throughout the city. Companies like Praha Bike, Rent a Bike Prague, and City Bike Prague offer a range of bicycles, including city bikes, mountain bikes, and electric bikes. Renting an electric bike can be a great option if you want to tackle Prague's hills with ease. Most rental shops provide maps and route suggestions, as well as helmets and locks.

When biking in Prague, it's important to follow the local traffic rules and be aware of your surroundings. Always ride in designated bike lanes where available and follow the same rules as motor vehicles when sharing the road. This includes stopping at red lights, signaling when turning, and yielding to pedestrians. Wearing a helmet is recommended for safety, although it is not required by law for adults.

One of the most popular biking routes in Prague is the Vltava River Path. This scenic route runs along the river and offers stunning views of the city's landmarks, including the Charles Bridge and the Dancing House. The path is mostly flat and well-paved, making it suitable for cyclists of all levels. Another great route is the trail through Stromovka Park, one of Prague's largest and most beautiful parks. The park's wide paths and lush greenery make it a pleasant place for a bike ride.

If you're feeling adventurous, you can also explore some of Prague's more challenging biking routes. For example, the trail up to Petrin Hill offers a rewarding workout and incredible views of the city from the top. Similarly, biking to the Prokop Valley nature reserve provides a mix of urban and natural scenery, with trails that wind through forests and past rocky cliffs.

Prague also offers guided bike tours for those who prefer a structured experience. These tours are led by experienced guides who can show you the best routes and provide insights into the city's history and culture. Options range from short city tours to full-day excursions that take you out of the city to explore the surrounding countryside.

Safety is a key consideration when biking in Prague. While the city is generally safe for cyclists, it's important to stay vigilant and follow basic safety precautions. Always lock your bike when leaving it unattended, use lights and reflectors when riding at night, and avoid busy streets during peak traffic hours if possible. Additionally, be cautious when riding on cobblestone streets or tram tracks, as these surfaces can be slippery and uneven.

Walking and biking are excellent ways to get around Prague and experience the city's unique charm. Walking allows you to explore at your own pace, discover hidden gems, and fully appreciate the city's stunning architecture. Biking offers a more active way to see the sights, with plenty of scenic routes and bike-friendly paths to choose from. Whether you prefer to walk or bike, both modes of transportation provide a flexible, enjoyable, and eco-friendly way to explore one of Europe's most beautiful cities.

CHAPTER 4

ACCOMMODATION OPTIONS IN PRAGUE

Best Areas to Stay in Prague

Choosing the best area to stay in Prague can significantly enhance your travel experience, as each neighborhood offers its own unique atmosphere, attractions, and conveniences. Understanding these differences will help you select the perfect location that aligns with your preferences and needs.

Staying in the Old Town (Staré Město) is a great choice if you want to be in the heart of Prague's historical and cultural scene. The Old Town is characterized by its narrow cobblestone streets, stunning Gothic and Baroque architecture, and numerous landmarks. The famous Old Town Square is a hub of activity, featuring the iconic Astronomical Clock and surrounded by beautiful buildings. From here, you can easily walk to Charles Bridge, one of Prague's most photographed sites. The area is filled with restaurants, cafes, shops, and museums, making it incredibly convenient for tourists. However, because of its central location and popularity, it can be quite busy and sometimes noisy, especially during peak tourist seasons.

Adjacent to the Old Town is the Lesser Town (Malá Strana), which lies across the Vltava River. This area offers a more tranquil atmosphere while still being close to major attractions. Lesser Town is known for its charming streets, beautiful gardens, and historical sites such as the Church of St. Nicholas and the Wallenstein Palace. One of the main highlights is Prague Castle, which dominates the skyline and offers panoramic views of the city. Staying in Lesser Town provides a quieter experience compared to the bustling Old Town, making it ideal for those who prefer a more relaxed environment while still being within walking distance to central attractions.

The New Town (Nové Město) is another excellent area to stay, especially for those who enjoy a lively and modern atmosphere. Established in the 14th century by Charles IV, the New Town is home to Wenceslas Square, a vibrant area filled with shops, restaurants, and nightlife. This neighborhood is a blend of historical and contemporary elements, offering a variety of cultural sites such as the National Museum and the State Opera. The New Town also provides easy access to public transportation, making it convenient for exploring other parts of Prague. This area is slightly less touristy than the Old Town, which can be a plus for those looking to experience a more local vibe.

For a more bohemian and artistic experience, the Vinohrady district is a great choice. Located just east of the New Town, Vinohrady is known for its Art Nouveau and Neo-

Renaissance architecture, tree-lined streets, and vibrant cultural scene. This neighborhood is popular among locals and expats, offering a plethora of trendy cafes, bars, and restaurants. Vinohrady is also home to several parks, including Riegrovy Sady, which offers beautiful views of Prague's skyline. Staying in Vinohrady provides a more residential feel, making it ideal for travelers who want to experience local life while still being close to the city center.

The neighborhood of Žižkov is another fantastic option, especially for budget-conscious travelers. Known for its lively nightlife and eclectic atmosphere, Žižkov is often referred to as Prague's most vibrant district. The area is home to the iconic Žižkov Television Tower, which offers an observation deck with panoramic views of the city. Žižkov has a wide range of accommodation options, from budget hostels to mid-range hotels. It's also well-connected by public transportation, allowing easy access to the rest of Prague. This neighborhood's unique character and affordable prices make it a popular choice among younger travelers and those looking for a more offbeat experience.

The district of Smíchov, located just south of Lesser Town, is another area worth considering. This neighborhood has undergone significant development in recent years and now boasts a mix of modern amenities and historical charm. Smíchov is home to the popular Anděl shopping area, which includes a large shopping mall, cinemas, and numerous dining options. The riverside location provides beautiful views and pleasant walking paths along the Vltava River. Smíchov's proximity to both the city center and the green spaces of Petřín Hill makes it an attractive option for travelers seeking convenience and variety.

Staying in the Holešovice district offers a unique blend of industrial history and contemporary culture. Once a primarily industrial area, Holešovice has transformed into a trendy neighborhood with art galleries, stylish cafes, and hip bars. The DOX Centre for Contemporary Art and the National Gallery's Veletržní Palace are major cultural attractions in this area. Holešovice also hosts several local markets, including the bustling Prague Market. This neighborhood provides a more laid-back atmosphere compared to the city center, making it a good choice for travelers interested in art, culture, and a less touristy experience.

Another appealing area is the district of Dejvice, located to the northwest of the city center. This neighborhood is known for its spacious streets, parks, and residential feel. Dejvice is home to several embassies and universities, giving it a cosmopolitan atmosphere. The area offers a mix of upscale and mid-range accommodations, along with a variety of restaurants and cafes. Staying in Dejvice provides easy access to Prague Castle and the surrounding green spaces, making it ideal for those who enjoy a quieter, more refined environment.

Understanding the distinct characteristics of each neighborhood will help you choose the best place to stay, ensuring a memorable and enjoyable visit to this enchanting city.

Luxury Hotels

Prague, with its rich history, stunning architecture, and vibrant cultural scene, is a city that attracts millions of visitors each year. For those looking to experience Prague in the utmost comfort and style, the city offers a range of luxury hotels that provide world-class accommodation and exceptional service.

One of the most iconic luxury hotels in Prague is the Four Seasons Hotel Prague. Located in the heart of the Old Town, this hotel offers stunning views of the Vltava River and Prague Castle. The Four Seasons Hotel Prague combines modern luxury with historic charm, featuring rooms and suites that are elegantly decorated with contemporary furnishings and historical accents. Guests can enjoy a range of amenities, including a full-service spa, a fitness center, and a fine-dining restaurant that serves both Czech and international cuisine. The hotel's prime location makes it an ideal base for exploring the city's major attractions, such as the Charles Bridge and the Old Town Square.

Another renowned luxury hotel is the Mandarin Oriental, Prague. Situated in a former monastery in the picturesque

Lesser Town, this hotel offers a unique blend of historical architecture and modern comforts. The Mandarin Oriental, Prague features spacious rooms and suites that are tastefully decorated with a mix of contemporary and traditional elements. The hotel's spa, located in a Renaissance chapel, provides a tranquil setting for relaxation and rejuvenation. Guests can also enjoy fine dining at the hotel's restaurant, which offers a menu inspired by both Czech and Asian cuisine. The hotel's location near Prague Castle and the beautiful gardens of Petřín Hill makes it a perfect choice for those looking to explore the city's historic sites.

For those seeking a truly opulent experience, the Augustine, a Luxury Collection Hotel, Prague, is an excellent option. This hotel is located in a complex of seven buildings, including a 13th-century Augustinian monastery. The Augustine offers luxurious rooms and suites that feature original architectural details, such as vaulted ceilings and wooden beams, combined with modern amenities. The hotel's courtyard garden provides a peaceful retreat, while the spa offers a range of treatments to pamper guests. The Augustine's restaurant serves contemporary European cuisine, with a focus on local ingredients. Its central location in Lesser Town provides easy access to many of Prague's top attractions, including St. Nicholas Church and the John Lennon Wall.

The Alchymist Grand Hotel and Spa is another exceptional luxury hotel in Prague. Housed in a Baroque-style building in the historic Lesser Town, this hotel exudes old-world charm and elegance. The Alchymist Grand Hotel and Spa features opulent rooms and suites that are richly decorated with antique furnishings, crystal chandeliers, and luxurious fabrics. The hotel's spa, located in a former cellar, offers a range of treatments, including massages, facials, and body wraps. Guests can enjoy fine dining at the hotel's restaurant, which serves Italian and Mediterranean cuisine. The hotel's proximity to Prague Castle and Charles Bridge makes it an ideal choice for those looking to explore the city's historic landmarks.

The Hotel Paris Prague is another top-tier luxury hotel that combines historic charm with modern amenities. Located near the Municipal House in the heart of the Old Town, this hotel is housed in a beautiful Art Nouveau building. The Hotel Paris Prague offers elegant rooms and suites that are decorated with period furnishings and modern conveniences. The hotel's wellness center includes a spa, a fitness room, and a sauna, providing a range of options for relaxation and fitness. The hotel's restaurant, Sarah Bernhardt, offers gourmet dining with a focus on French and Czech cuisine. Its central location provides easy access to many of Prague's main attractions, including Wenceslas Square and the Old Town Square.

The Grand Hotel Bohemia is another excellent choice for luxury accommodation in Prague. Situated in the heart of the Old Town, this hotel offers a blend of traditional elegance and modern comfort. The Grand Hotel Bohemia features stylish rooms and suites that are equipped with the latest amenities, ensuring a comfortable and luxurious stay. The hotel's restaurant, Franz Josef, serves a variety of Czech and international dishes, while the hotel's bar offers a selection of fine wines and cocktails. The hotel's central location makes it an ideal base for exploring the city, with many of Prague's top attractions within walking distance.

For a unique and contemporary luxury experience, the Design Hotel Jewel Prague is a great option. This boutique hotel is located in a historic building in the heart of the Old Town, offering a stylish and intimate atmosphere. The Design Hotel Jewel Prague features individually decorated rooms that combine modern design with traditional elements. The hotel's restaurant and bar provide a cozy setting for enjoying a meal or a drink, with a menu that focuses on local and seasonal ingredients. The hotel's central location allows guests to easily explore the city's main attractions, including the Old Town Square and the Charles Bridge.

By choosing one of these top-tier luxury hotels, you can ensure a comfortable and memorable stay in one of Europe's most beautiful and historic cities. Each of these hotels provides exceptional service, luxurious accommodations, and prime locations, making them ideal choices for discerning travelers seeking the best that Prague has to offer.

Boutique Hotels

Prague, with its rich history, vibrant culture, and stunning architecture, is a city that offers a variety of accommodation options to suit different tastes and preferences. Boutique hotels, in particular, provide a unique and intimate experience that is often characterized by personalized service, stylish décor, and a sense of individuality that larger hotels may lack.

The Golden Well Hotel, or U Zlaté Studně, is a highly acclaimed boutique hotel located near Prague Castle. This charming hotel offers a tranquil and luxurious retreat with stunning views of the city. The Golden Well Hotel is housed in a historic building that dates back to the 16th century, and it has preserved many of its original architectural details. The rooms and suites are elegantly decorated with a blend of antique furnishings and modern amenities. Guests can enjoy a complimentary breakfast, afternoon tea, and a nightly turn-down service with chocolates and a weather forecast. The hotel's restaurant, Terasa U Zlaté Studně, is renowned for its gourmet cuisine and offers a terrace with panoramic views of Prague.

The Alchymist Grand Hotel and Spa is another exquisite boutique hotel in Prague. Situated in the picturesque Lesser Town, this hotel is housed in a Baroque-style building that exudes old-world charm and elegance. The Alchymist Grand Hotel and Spa features opulent rooms and suites that are richly decorated with antique furnishings, crystal chandeliers, and luxurious fabrics. The hotel's spa, located in a former cellar, offers a range of treatments, including massages, facials, and body wraps. Guests can enjoy fine dining at the hotel's restaurant, which serves Italian and Mediterranean cuisine. The hotel's proximity to Prague Castle and Charles Bridge makes it an ideal choice for those looking to explore the city's historic landmarks.

Located in the heart of the Old Town, the Ventana Hotel Prague is a boutique hotel that offers a blend of luxury and comfort. This hotel is housed in a historic building that combines Neo-Gothic and Art Nouveau architectural styles. The Ventana Hotel Prague features spacious rooms and suites that are tastefully decorated with elegant furnishings and modern amenities. Guests can enjoy a complimentary breakfast buffet in the hotel's stylish dining room, and the Ventana Bar offers a cozy setting for evening drinks. The hotel's central location provides easy access to many of Prague's main attractions, including the Old Town Square, the Astronomical Clock, and the Týn Church.

The Hotel Josef is a contemporary boutique hotel that stands out for its sleek and modern design. Located in the Jewish Quarter, this hotel offers a stylish and sophisticated atmosphere. The Hotel Josef features rooms and suites that are decorated with clean lines, minimalist furnishings, and large windows that let in plenty of natural light. The hotel's rooftop terrace provides stunning views of the city, and the on-site fitness center is well-equipped for guests who want to stay active during their stay. The Hotel Josef also offers a complimentary breakfast buffet with a variety of healthy and delicious options. Its central location makes it an excellent base for exploring Prague's cultural and historical sites.

The Aria Hotel Prague is a unique boutique hotel that caters to music lovers. Each floor of the hotel is dedicated to a different musical genre, and the rooms and suites are themed around famous composers and musicians. The Aria Hotel Prague offers a range of amenities, including a music library, a private screening room, and access to the Vrtba Garden, a UNESCO World Heritage site. The hotel's restaurant, Coda, serves gourmet cuisine with a focus on seasonal and local ingredients. Guests can also enjoy live music performances in the hotel's elegant lounge. The Aria Hotel Prague's location in the Lesser Town provides easy access to many of Prague's top attractions, including Prague Castle and St. Nicholas Church.

The ICON Hotel & Lounge is a trendy boutique hotel located in the New Town. This hotel offers a contemporary and stylish atmosphere with a focus on comfort and design. The ICON Hotel & Lounge features rooms and suites that are decorated with modern furnishings, luxurious beds, and high-quality linens. The hotel's restaurant, ROOM, serves a delicious breakfast buffet and offers a menu of international dishes for lunch and dinner. The ICON Hotel & Lounge also features a Thai massage studio, providing a relaxing retreat for guests. Its central location near Wenceslas Square makes it a convenient choice for exploring Prague's shopping, dining, and entertainment options.

The Hotel Pod Věží is a charming boutique hotel located near the Charles Bridge in the Lesser Town. This hotel is housed in two historic buildings and offers a warm and welcoming atmosphere. The Hotel Pod Věží features rooms and suites that are elegantly decorated with a mix of traditional and modern furnishings. Guests can enjoy a complimentary breakfast buffet, and the hotel's restaurant serves a variety of Czech and international dishes. The hotel's location near the Charles Bridge provides easy access to many of Prague's main attractions, including Prague Castle and the Old Town.

In conclusion, Prague offers a diverse range of boutique hotels that cater to different tastes and preferences. Whether you are looking for a historic hotel with old-world charm, a modern hotel with contemporary design, or a unique hotel with a thematic focus, Prague has something to offer. By choosing one of these top-tier boutique hotels, you can ensure a comfortable and memorable stay in one of Europe's most beautiful and historic cities. Each of these hotels provides exceptional service, luxurious accommodations, and prime locations, making them ideal choices for discerning travelers seeking the best that Prague has to offer.

Budget Hotels and Hostels

Prague is a city that offers a wide range of accommodation options to suit all budgets, making it an attractive destination for travelers from all walks of life. For those seeking affordable lodging without compromising on comfort and convenience, Prague has an array of budget hotels and hostels that provide excellent value for money.

One of the most popular budget accommodation options in Prague is the Hostel One Prague. Located in the vibrant neighborhood of Žižkov, this hostel is known for its friendly atmosphere and social environment. Hostel One Prague offers a variety of dormitory and private rooms, all of which are clean and comfortable. The hostel provides free Wi-Fi, a fully equipped kitchen, and a cozy common area where guests can relax and meet fellow travelers. Additionally, the hostel organizes daily activities and events, such as city tours and pub crawls, which are great for those looking to explore Prague and make new friends. Its location in Žižkov means that guests are close to numerous bars, restaurants, and cafes, as well as public transportation links to the city center.

Another excellent budget option is the Czech Inn Hostel, which offers both hostel and hotel-style accommodations. Situated in the Vinohrady district, the Czech Inn is housed in a beautifully restored 19th-century building. The hostel features a range of room types, including shared dormitories, private rooms, and apartments, catering to different budgets and preferences. The Czech Inn provides modern amenities such as free Wi-Fi, a bar, and a café that serves breakfast and snacks. The hostel also offers guided tours and activities, making it easy for guests to explore the city. Vinohrady is known for its vibrant nightlife, parks, and trendy eateries, making it an excellent location for travelers who want to experience local culture.

The Sir Toby's Hostel is another fantastic budget accommodation option in Prague. Located in the Holešovice district, Sir Toby's Hostel is known for its charming and eclectic décor. The hostel offers a variety of room types, including dormitories, private rooms, and family rooms. Guests can enjoy amenities such as free Wi-Fi, a fully equipped kitchen, a garden, and a cozy common room with a fireplace. Sir Toby's Hostel also has an on-site pub that serves local beers and hosts regular events like quiz nights and live music. The Holešovice district is a trendy area with art galleries, cafes, and markets, and it is well-connected to the city center by public transportation.

For travelers looking for a central location, the Old Prague Hostel is an excellent choice. Situated in the heart of the Old Town, this hostel is within walking distance of major attractions such as the Old Town Square, the Astronomical Clock, and Charles Bridge. The Old Prague Hostel offers a range of dormitory and private rooms, all of which are clean and comfortable. The hostel provides free breakfast, free Wi-Fi, and a communal kitchen for guests to use. There is also a common area where guests can relax and socialize. The central location means that guests have easy access to numerous restaurants, bars, and shops, as well as public transportation links to other parts of the city.

The Hostel Downtown is another highly recommended budget accommodation option in Prague. Located in the New Town, this hostel is just a short walk from Wenceslas Square and the National Museum. Hostel Downtown offers a variety of room types, including dormitories and private rooms, all of which are spacious and well-maintained. The hostel provides free Wi-Fi, a fully equipped kitchen, and a common room with games and books. Hostel Downtown also organizes daily activities, such as city tours, cooking classes, and movie nights, making it a great choice for solo travelers and those looking to meet new people. The New Town is a lively area with plenty of dining and entertainment options, as well as excellent public transportation links.

The Sophie's Hostel is a stylish and affordable option located in the New Town. This boutique hostel offers a range of accommodations, including shared dormitories, private rooms, and apartments. Sophie's Hostel is known for its chic and modern design, with rooms that are bright and spacious. The hostel provides free Wi-Fi, a communal kitchen, and a breakfast buffet with a variety of options. There is also a cozy café on-site that serves coffee and snacks throughout the day. Sophie's Hostel offers guided tours and activities, helping guests to explore Prague and connect with other travelers. Its central location provides easy access to many of Prague's main attractions and public transportation.

For those seeking a more traditional hotel experience on a budget, the Hotel Merkur is an excellent choice. Located near the Florenc bus and metro station, Hotel Merkur offers comfortable and affordable accommodations in a convenient location. The hotel features a range of room types, including single, double, and family rooms, all of which are clean and well-appointed. Guests can enjoy amenities such as free Wi-Fi, a complimentary breakfast buffet, and a 24-hour front desk. The hotel's central location means that guests are within walking distance of many attractions, including the Old Town Square and Wenceslas Square, as well as numerous restaurants and shops.

The B&B Hotel Prague City is another great budget hotel option. Situated in the Florenc district, this hotel offers modern and comfortable accommodations at an affordable price. The B&B Hotel Prague City features a variety of room types, including single, double, and family rooms, all of which are equipped with modern amenities such as free Wi-Fi, air conditioning, and flat-screen TVs. The hotel provides a complimentary breakfast buffet and has a 24-hour reception desk. Its location near the Florenc bus and metro station makes it easy to explore Prague and reach other parts of the city.

By choosing one of these recommended budget accommodations, you can enjoy a comfortable and memorable stay in one of Europe's most beautiful and historic cities. Each of these options provides a unique experience, with clean and comfortable rooms, modern amenities, and convenient locations, making them ideal choices for budget-conscious travelers seeking the best that Prague has to offer.

Apartments and Vacation Rentals

Prague, with its enchanting architecture and rich cultural heritage, offers a variety of accommodation options that cater to diverse preferences and budgets. Among these, apartments and vacation rentals stand out as excellent choices for travelers seeking the comfort of home combined with the flexibility and convenience of a self-catered stay.

Choosing to stay in an apartment or vacation rental in Prague allows you to experience the city like a local. One of the main advantages of these accommodations is the space they offer compared to traditional hotel rooms. Apartments typically come with separate living and sleeping areas, fully equipped kitchens, and often additional amenities such as washing machines and private balconies. This setup is particularly beneficial for families, groups of friends, or travelers planning an extended stay, as it provides the flexibility to cook your own meals, do laundry, and enjoy more living space.

In the heart of Prague's Old Town, you will find a range of beautifully appointed apartments that offer both historical charm and modern conveniences. For example, the Old Town Square Apartments provide spacious and elegantly furnished units that are just steps away from the iconic Astronomical Clock and other major attractions. These apartments feature high ceilings, large windows, and tasteful decor that blends traditional and contemporary elements. Staying here means you can immerse yourself in the vibrant atmosphere of the Old Town, with its numerous restaurants, cafes, and shops.

Another excellent option in the Old Town is the Residence Karolina. This complex offers luxurious apartments with modern amenities, including fully equipped kitchens, high-speed Wi-Fi, and flat-screen TVs. The Residence Karolina is located within walking distance of the Charles Bridge and Wenceslas Square, making it an ideal base for exploring the city. The building itself is a beautifully restored historical property, providing a blend of old-world elegance and modern comfort.

For those looking to stay in the Lesser Town (Malá Strana), the Lesser Town Square Apartments are a fantastic choice. These apartments are housed in a historical building overlooking the picturesque square and are close to major landmarks such as Prague Castle and St. Nicholas Church. The units are spacious and well-appointed, with features like hardwood floors, antique furnishings, and modern kitchens.

This location offers a quieter and more relaxed atmosphere compared to the bustling Old Town, making it perfect for those seeking a peaceful retreat while still being close to key attractions.

The Vinohrady district is another popular area for vacation rentals, known for its beautiful residential streets, parks, and vibrant dining scene. The Vinohrady Boutique Apartments offer stylish and comfortable accommodations in this charming neighborhood. These apartments are designed with a contemporary flair, featuring open-plan living spaces, modern kitchens, and elegant furnishings. The location is ideal for those who want to experience Prague's local culture, with plenty of trendy cafes, bars, and restaurants nearby.

For travelers seeking budget-friendly options, the Žižkov district offers a range of affordable apartments and vacation rentals. The Prague Central Apartments in Žižkov provide clean and comfortable units with essential amenities such as Wi-Fi, kitchenettes, and washing machines. The area is known for its lively nightlife and eclectic atmosphere, with many local pubs, clubs, and cultural venues. Staying in Žižkov gives you the opportunity to explore a more off-the-beaten-path side of Prague while still being just a short tram ride away from the city center.

Another great budget option is the City Centre Apartments in the New Town. These apartments offer simple yet functional accommodations that are perfect for travelers on a budget. The units include kitchenettes, comfortable beds, and free Wi-Fi. The New Town is a vibrant area with a mix of historical and modern attractions, including Wenceslas Square, the National Museum, and various shopping and dining options. The central location ensures that you can easily explore all that Prague has to offer.

For a unique and luxurious experience, consider staying in one of Prague's penthouse apartments. The Charles Bridge Penthouse Apartments offer stunning views of the Charles Bridge and the Vltava River from private terraces. These high-end units are beautifully designed with spacious living areas, modern kitchens, and luxurious bathrooms. The prime location in the heart of Prague's historical center makes these penthouses an excellent choice for those looking to indulge in luxury while enjoying breathtaking views of the city's landmarks.

Another luxurious option is the Prague Castle View Apartments, which provide an unparalleled view of Prague Castle from their windows and balconies. These apartments are elegantly furnished with high-end amenities, including fully equipped kitchens, spacious living areas, and stylish decor. Staying here allows you to wake up to the sight of one of Prague's most iconic landmarks and enjoy the convenience of being close to major attractions and cultural sites.

For travelers who value privacy and independence, vacation rentals such as townhouses or entire homes are also available in Prague. These rentals provide the ultimate in space and flexibility, often featuring multiple bedrooms, private gardens, and ample living space. They are ideal for families or groups of friends looking to stay together in a comfortable and private setting. Properties like the Luxury Family House in Prague offer all the comforts of home, including fully equipped kitchens, outdoor spaces, and modern amenities, making them perfect for extended stays or special occasions.

Staying in an apartment or vacation rental allows you to experience the city like a local, with the added benefits of space, flexibility, and the comforts of home. By choosing one of these recommended accommodation options, you can ensure a comfortable and memorable stay in one of Europe's most beautiful and historic cities. Each of these options provides unique features and amenities, making them ideal choices for travelers seeking the best that Prague has to offer.

Unique Stays

Prague, renowned for its historical charm and stunning architecture, offers a myriad of unique accommodation options that allow visitors to experience the city in an extraordinary way. These distinctive stays range from historic castles and luxurious houseboats to artistically designed hotels and themed apartments.

One of the most remarkable places to stay in Prague is the Augustine, a Luxury Collection Hotel. This hotel is housed in a former Augustinian monastery dating back to the 13th century, offering a rare blend of history and luxury. The Augustine's rooms and suites are individually designed, featuring original architectural details such as vaulted ceilings and wooden beams, combined with contemporary furnishings. Guests can explore the monastery's cloistered terraces, hidden garden, and a 17th-century library. The hotel's restaurant serves gourmet dishes inspired by Czech cuisine, and the Augustine Spa provides a tranquil retreat with a range of treatments. Its location in the Lesser Town, near Prague Castle, makes it ideal for exploring the city's historical sites.

Another unique accommodation option is the Hotel U Zlaté Studně, or the Golden Well Hotel, which offers an intimate and luxurious stay near Prague Castle. This boutique hotel is located in a Renaissance building that once belonged to Emperor Rudolf II's astrologer, Tycho Brahe. The Golden Well Hotel provides stunning views of the city and features elegantly appointed rooms with period furnishings and modern amenities. The hotel's restaurant, Terasa U Zlaté Studně, is renowned for its fine dining and breathtaking views of Prague. Guests can also enjoy a private entrance to the Royal Gardens of Prague Castle, adding to the exclusivity and charm of their stay.

For a truly unconventional experience, consider staying on a houseboat on the Vltava River. The Houseboat Rohan Boat Prague offers a unique and memorable stay with the added allure of being on the water. These houseboats are fully equipped with modern amenities, including kitchens, bathrooms, and comfortable living spaces. Guests can enjoy the serene river views, relax on the deck, and even fish from the boat. Staying on a houseboat provides a different perspective of Prague, allowing you to wake up to the gentle sounds of the river and take in the city's skyline from a unique vantage point.

The Dancing House Hotel is another distinctive accommodation option that stands out for its architectural design. Located in the famous Dancing House building designed by architects Frank Gehry and Vlado Milunić, this hotel offers a modern and artistic stay in the heart of Prague. The rooms are stylishly decorated with contemporary furnishings and offer stunning views of the Vltava River and the city. The hotel's rooftop terrace and bar provide panoramic views of Prague, making it an ideal spot to enjoy a drink and watch the sunset. Staying at the Dancing House Hotel allows guests to experience one of Prague's most iconic and innovative buildings.

For travelers interested in an artistically inspired stay, the Art Hotel Prague is an excellent choice. Located in the quiet residential neighborhood of Letná, this boutique hotel is surrounded by parks and offers easy access to Prague's cultural attractions. The Art Hotel Prague features rooms and suites that are individually decorated with original artworks by contemporary Czech artists. The hotel's gallery-like atmosphere creates a unique and creative ambiance. Guests can enjoy a complimentary breakfast, relax in the hotel's garden, and explore the nearby Letná Park and National Gallery. The Art Hotel Prague provides a peaceful and artistic retreat while still being close to the city center.

The Vintage Design Hotel Sax is another exceptional option for those seeking a unique and stylish stay. Situated in the Lesser Town, this boutique hotel is renowned for its retro-inspired design, featuring mid-century modern furniture and decor. The rooms are bright and colorful, with each one uniquely decorated to reflect a different aspect of vintage style. The hotel's lounge and bar continue the retro theme, providing a cozy and nostalgic atmosphere. Guests can enjoy a range of amenities, including a fitness center, a spa, and a complimentary breakfast. The Vintage Design Hotel Sax's central location makes it easy to explore Prague's historical landmarks, such as Charles Bridge and St. Nicholas Church.

For a more whimsical experience, consider staying at the Hotel & Residence At The Black Star. This charming hotel is located in a Gothic building in the Old Town, featuring a mix of historical and fantastical elements. The rooms are decorated with antique furnishings, rich fabrics, and unique touches such as hand-painted murals and canopy beds. The hotel's central location, just a short walk from the Old Town

Square and the Astronomical Clock, makes it an ideal base for exploring Prague's historic center. The Hotel & Residence At The Black Star provides a magical and enchanting stay that transports guests to a different era.

The Hotel Pod Věží is another unique accommodation option that combines historical charm with modern comfort. Located near the Charles Bridge in the Lesser Town, this hotel is housed in two historic buildings and offers beautifully decorated rooms with a blend of traditional and contemporary furnishings. Guests can enjoy a complimentary breakfast, dine at the hotel's restaurant, and explore the picturesque surroundings of the Lesser Town. The Hotel Pod Věží's proximity to major attractions such as Prague Castle and the Old Town makes it an excellent choice for travelers who want to experience the best of Prague's history and culture.

By choosing one of these unique stays, you can ensure a truly exceptional and enriching visit to one of Europe's most beautiful and historic cities.

CHAPTER 5

TOP ATTRACTIONS IN PRAGUE

Iconic Landmarks

Prague, the capital city of the Czech Republic, is renowned for its rich history, stunning architecture, and cultural heritage. It is a city that captivates visitors with its blend of Gothic, Baroque, and Renaissance buildings, each telling a story of the past.

One of the most famous landmarks in Prague is the Charles Bridge (Karlův most). This historic bridge, completed in 1402, spans the Vltava River and connects the Old Town with the Lesser Town. The bridge is adorned with 30 statues of saints, each with its own story and significance. The most notable statues include those of St. John of Nepomuk, St. Luthgard, and St. Adalbert. Walking across the Charles Bridge is like stepping back in time, with its cobblestone pathway and medieval towers at each end. The bridge is a popular spot for both locals and tourists, offering stunning views of the river and the city's skyline, especially at sunrise and sunset.

Prague Castle (Pražský hrad) is another iconic landmark that dominates the city's skyline. This vast complex, founded in the 9th century, is one of the largest castles in the world. It has been the seat of Czech kings, emperors, and presidents for over a thousand years. The castle complex includes several buildings of historical and architectural significance, such as the Gothic-style St. Vitus Cathedral, the Old Royal Palace, and the Basilica of St. George. St. Vitus Cathedral, with its towering spires and intricate stained glass windows, is the most prominent structure within the castle grounds. Visitors can explore the castle's courtyards, gardens, and museums, which house a collection of Bohemian crown jewels, historical artifacts, and artworks. The changing of the guard ceremony, held every hour, is a popular attraction for tourists.

The Old Town Square (Staroměstské náměstí) is the heart of Prague's historic center. This bustling square is surrounded by colorful buildings, each with its own unique architectural style. The Old Town Hall, with its famous Astronomical Clock (Orloj), is a highlight of the square. The clock, installed in 1410, is one of the oldest astronomical clocks in the world that is still in operation. Every hour, the clock puts on a show, featuring a procession of the Twelve Apostles and other figures. The square is also home to the Gothic Church of Our Lady before Týn, with its distinctive twin spires, and the Baroque-style St. Nicholas Church. Throughout the year, the Old Town Square hosts various events, including the traditional Christmas and Easter markets, where visitors can enjoy festive foods, crafts, and entertainment.

The Dancing House (Tančící dům) is a modern architectural landmark in Prague. Designed by architects Frank Gehry and Vlado Milunić, this unique building, completed in 1996, stands out amidst the city's historic architecture. The Dancing House, also known as "Fred and Ginger" because its design resembles a dancing couple, is an example of deconstructivist architecture. The building houses offices, a restaurant with panoramic views, and a gallery. Its innovative design and striking appearance make it a must-see for architecture enthusiasts.

The Jewish Quarter (Josefov) is a significant historical and cultural area in Prague. This district, named after Emperor Joseph II, who implemented reforms that improved the living conditions of Jews in the late 18th century, is home to several important landmarks. The Old Jewish Cemetery, dating back to the 15th century, is one of the oldest Jewish burial sites in Europe. It contains thousands of graves and is a poignant reminder of the Jewish community's history in Prague. The Jewish Museum in Prague, which includes six synagogues and other historical buildings, offers a comprehensive look at Jewish heritage and traditions. The Spanish Synagogue, with its stunning Moorish Revival interior, and the Old-New Synagogue, one of the oldest active synagogues in Europe, are notable highlights of the Jewish Quarter.

Wenceslas Square (Václavské náměstí) is a vibrant and historic square in the New Town. Named after Saint

Wenceslas, the patron saint of Bohemia, this square has been the site of many significant events in Czech history, including political demonstrations and celebrations. The square is lined with shops, cafes, and restaurants, making it a popular destination for both locals and tourists. At the top of the square stands the National Museum, an imposing Neo-Renaissance building that houses a vast collection of natural history, art, and cultural artifacts. The statue of Saint Wenceslas on horseback, located in front of the museum, is a well-known meeting point and symbol of Czech national pride.

The Powder Tower (Prašná brána) is one of the original city gates of Prague, dating back to the 15th century. This Gothic tower, once used to store gunpowder, now serves as an entrance to the Old Town from the New Town. Visitors can climb the tower's 186 steps to reach the viewing gallery, which offers panoramic views of the city's historic center. The Powder Tower is an excellent example of Prague's medieval architecture and its role in the city's fortifications.

The Vyšehrad Fortress is another significant historical site in Prague. Located on a hill overlooking the Vltava River, Vyšehrad is a former royal residence and fortress with roots dating back to the 10th century. The complex includes the Basilica of St. Peter and St. Paul, with its striking twin spires and beautiful interior, and the Vyšehrad Cemetery, the final resting place of many notable Czech figures, including composer Antonín Dvořák and writer Karel Čapek. The fortress grounds also feature parkland, walking paths, and ruins of medieval structures, providing a serene and picturesque setting.

Petrin Hill (Petřín) is a green oasis in the heart of Prague, offering stunning views of the city. The hill is home to several attractions, including the Petrin Lookout Tower, which resembles a mini Eiffel Tower. Visitors can climb the 299 steps to the top of the tower for panoramic views of Prague. The hill also features the Mirror Maze, a fun and family-friendly attraction, and the Rose Garden, which is particularly beautiful in the spring and summer. The Hunger Wall, a medieval fortification built during the reign of Charles IV, runs along the hill and adds to its historical significance.

From the medieval Charles Bridge and the majestic Prague Castle to the vibrant Old Town Square and the modern Dancing House, each landmark offers a unique glimpse into the city's past and present. Exploring these landmarks provides visitors with a deeper understanding of Prague's significance as a historical and cultural center in Europe. By visiting these iconic sites, you can fully appreciate the beauty and charm of this remarkable city.

Museums and Galleries

Prague, with its rich history and vibrant cultural scene, is home to a wide array of museums and galleries that offer deep insights into the city's past, present, and future. These institutions house extensive collections of art, artifacts, and historical documents, providing a comprehensive overview of Prague's cultural and artistic heritage.

The National Museum (Národní muzeum) is the largest and one of the most important museums in Prague. Founded in 1818, the museum is housed in a grand Neo-Renaissance building located at the top of Wenceslas Square. The National Museum's extensive collection spans natural history, anthropology, archaeology, art, and music. The museum's exhibits include fossils, minerals, and taxidermy specimens, as well as artifacts from prehistoric times to the present day. The museum also features a vast collection of Czech and Slovak historical documents, providing valuable insights into the country's history. The recently renovated building itself is a marvel, with its grand staircase, intricate ceiling frescoes, and impressive dome offering breathtaking views of the city.

The Prague Castle complex is home to several important museums, including the Lobkowicz Palace Museum. This museum, housed in a beautifully restored Baroque palace, showcases the private art collection of the Lobkowicz family. The collection includes works by renowned artists such as Canaletto, Bruegel, and Velázquez, as well as historical musical instruments, manuscripts, and decorative arts. Highlights of the museum include original scores and manuscripts by Beethoven and Mozart. The museum also offers an audio guide narrated by members of the Lobkowicz family, providing personal insights into the collection's history and significance.

The Jewish Museum in Prague is one of the oldest and most comprehensive Jewish museums in the world. Founded in 1906, the museum comprises several historic synagogues, the Old Jewish Cemetery, and the Ceremonial Hall. The museum's extensive collection includes religious artifacts, manuscripts, and textiles that chronicle the history and culture of the Jewish community in Prague and Bohemia. The Spanish Synagogue, with its stunning Moorish Revival architecture, houses exhibits on the history of Jews in the Czech Republic from the emancipation in the 19th century to the present day. The Old Jewish Cemetery, dating back to the 15th century, is one of the most significant Jewish burial sites in Europe and provides a poignant insight into the Jewish community's history.

The National Gallery in Prague (Národní galerie v Praze) is another major cultural institution, comprising several historic buildings that house a vast collection of art. The gallery's main venues include the Trade Fair Palace (Veletržní palác), the Convent of St. Agnes of Bohemia (Anežský klášter), and the Kinský Palace (Palác Kinských). The Trade Fair Palace is home to the gallery's modern and contemporary art collections, featuring works by Czech and international artists such as Picasso, Klimt, and Mucha. The Convent of St. Agnes of Bohemia houses the gallery's medieval art collection, including stunning altarpieces and sculptures. The Kinský Palace showcases the gallery's collection of Asian art, with exhibits ranging from ancient Chinese ceramics to contemporary Japanese prints.

The Mucha Museum is dedicated to the life and work of Alphonse Mucha, one of the most famous Czech artists and a key figure in the Art Nouveau movement. The museum, located in the Baroque Kaunický Palace, features an extensive collection of Mucha's posters, paintings, photographs, and personal memorabilia. Highlights of the museum include Mucha's iconic posters for Sarah Bernhardt's theatrical productions and his monumental series of paintings, The Slav Epic, which depicts the history of the Slavic people. The museum provides a comprehensive overview of Mucha's artistic career and his contributions to the Art Nouveau style.

The Museum of Decorative Arts (Uměleckoprůmyslové museum) in Prague offers an extensive collection of decorative and applied arts, including glass, ceramics, textiles, furniture, and fashion. The museum's exhibits showcase the development of decorative arts from the Renaissance to the present day, with a particular emphasis on Czech and Central European design. The museum's glass collection is especially noteworthy, featuring exquisite examples of Bohemian glass and contemporary glass art. The museum also houses a comprehensive collection of photography, including works by Czech photographers such as Josef Sudek and František Drtikol.

The Kampa Museum, located on Kampa Island in the Lesser Town, is dedicated to modern and contemporary art. The museum's collection includes works by Central European artists such as František Kupka, Otto Gutfreund, and Jiří Kolář. The museum's striking modernist building, formerly a mill, offers stunning views of the Vltava River and the Charles Bridge. The Kampa Museum also hosts temporary exhibitions featuring contemporary artists from around the world, making it a dynamic and engaging cultural venue.

The Museum of Communism offers a unique and thought-provoking look at the history of communism in Czechoslovakia. The museum's exhibits cover the period from the Communist coup in 1948 to the Velvet Revolution in 1989, providing a comprehensive overview of life under the communist regime. The museum features a range of artifacts, including propaganda posters, uniforms, and everyday items from the communist era. The exhibits are accompanied by detailed explanations and personal stories, offering a nuanced and insightful perspective on this pivotal period in Czech history.

The Franz Kafka Museum, located in the Lesser Town, is dedicated to the life and work of one of Prague's most famous literary figures. The museum's exhibits include first editions of Kafka's works, personal letters, and photographs, as well as audiovisual displays that provide a deeper understanding of Kafka's writing and his connection to Prague. The museum's atmospheric setting, housed in a former brickworks, enhances the experience, immersing visitors in Kafka's world.

The DOX Centre for Contemporary Art, located in the Holešovice district, is one of Prague's leading venues for contemporary art. The center's innovative exhibitions feature works by both Czech and international artists, covering a wide range of media, including painting, sculpture, photography, and video. The DOX Centre also hosts a variety of cultural events, including lectures, workshops, and performances, making it a vibrant and dynamic cultural hub.

By visiting these institutions, you can gain a deeper understanding of Prague's past and present, making your visit to this beautiful and historic city truly memorable.

Parks and Gardens

Prague, known for its rich history and stunning architecture, is also home to an array of beautiful parks and gardens that offer a tranquil escape from the bustling city. These green spaces provide not only a place to relax and enjoy nature but also an opportunity to delve into the cultural and historical aspects of the city.

Letná Park (Letenské sady) is one of Prague's most beloved parks, offering expansive green spaces and breathtaking views of the city. Situated on Letná Hill, this park overlooks the Vltava River and provides panoramic views of the Old Town, making it a popular spot for both locals and tourists. Letná Park is known for its wide, tree-lined avenues, perfect for leisurely walks, cycling, or rollerblading. The park is also home to the iconic Metronome, a large kinetic sculpture that has become a symbol of the city. Originally, the site was occupied by a massive statue of Stalin, which was demolished in 1962. Today, the Metronome stands as a reminder of the city's past and a symbol of its progress. Letná Park also features several beer gardens, where visitors can enjoy a refreshing drink while taking in the stunning views.

Stromovka Park (Královská obora) is another significant green space in Prague, known for its lush greenery and serene atmosphere. Originally established as a royal game reserve in the 13th century, Stromovka Park has evolved into a public park that offers a peaceful retreat from the city. The park is characterized by its vast lawns, mature trees, and picturesque ponds, making it an ideal spot for picnicking, jogging, or simply relaxing. Stromovka also features a network of well-maintained paths, perfect for walking or cycling. The park is home to several historical buildings, including the Governor's Summer Palace, which now houses the National Museum of Agriculture. Additionally, the park hosts various cultural and recreational events throughout the year, attracting visitors of all ages.

Petrin Hill (Petřín) is one of Prague's most iconic green spaces, offering a blend of natural beauty and historical landmarks. The hill is covered with forests, gardens, and orchards, providing a lush and tranquil environment. One of the main attractions on Petrin Hill is the Petrin Lookout Tower, a miniature version of the Eiffel Tower, which offers panoramic views of Prague from its observation deck. Visitors can either climb the 299 steps to the top or take a funicular railway to reach the hill's summit. Petrin Hill is also home to the Mirror Maze, a fun and family-friendly attraction, and the Hunger Wall, a medieval fortification built during the reign of Charles IV. The Rose Garden on Petrin Hill is particularly beautiful in the spring and summer, with its vibrant blooms and fragrant scents.

Vyšehrad is another significant historical site that offers beautiful green spaces and stunning views of Prague. Located on a hill overlooking the Vltava River, Vyšehrad is a former royal residence and fortress with roots dating back to the 10th century. The complex includes several historical buildings, such as the Basilica of St. Peter and St. Paul, with its striking twin spires and beautiful interior, and the Vyšehrad Cemetery, the final resting place of many notable Czech figures, including composer Antonín Dvořák and writer Karel Čapek. The fortress grounds also feature parkland, walking paths, and ruins of medieval structures, providing a serene and picturesque setting. Vyšehrad's elevated position offers breathtaking views of the city and the river, making it a popular spot for picnicking and leisurely strolls.

Riegrovy Sady is a popular park located in the Vinohrady district, known for its beautiful views of Prague Castle and its vibrant social scene. The park features expansive lawns, mature trees, and a network of paths that are perfect for walking or jogging. Riegrovy Sady is also home to several beer gardens, where visitors can enjoy a drink while taking in the stunning views of the city. The park's elevated position provides an excellent vantage point for watching the sunset over Prague, making it a favorite spot for both locals and tourists. Riegrovy Sady also hosts various cultural and recreational events throughout the year, attracting a diverse crowd of visitors.

The Wallenstein Garden (Valdštejnská zahrada) is a beautifully landscaped Baroque garden located in the Lesser Town, adjacent to the Wallenstein Palace. The garden, designed in the early 17th century, features meticulously manicured lawns, ornamental flower beds, and a series of elegant statues and fountains. One of the garden's highlights is the impressive sala terrena, a grand open-air pavilion decorated with frescoes and stucco work. The Wallenstein Garden also includes a tranquil pond, home to several species of fish and waterfowl, and an aviary with a variety of exotic birds. The garden provides a peaceful retreat in the heart of the city, offering a serene and picturesque setting for relaxation and contemplation.

Vrtba Garden (Vrtbovská zahrada) is another exquisite Baroque garden, located on the slopes of Petrin Hill in the Lesser Town. The garden, designed in the early 18th century, is renowned for its terraced layout, elaborate statues, and stunning views of Prague. Vrtba Garden features a series of interconnected terraces, each adorned with meticulously maintained flower beds, hedges, and sculptures. The garden's upper terraces offer breathtaking views of the city, including the spires of St. Nicholas Church and Prague Castle. Vrtba Garden is a hidden gem, providing a tranquil and elegant setting for visitors to enjoy the beauty of Baroque landscape design.

The Franciscan Garden (Františkánská zahrada) is a peaceful oasis located in the New Town, just a short walk from Wenceslas Square. The garden, originally part of a Franciscan monastery, features a series of beautifully landscaped flower beds, lawns, and trees. The Franciscan Garden is known for its serene atmosphere and well-maintained paths, making it an ideal spot for a leisurely stroll or a moment of quiet reflection. The garden also includes a children's playground, providing a safe and enjoyable space for families. The Franciscan Garden's central location makes it a convenient and accessible green space in the heart of Prague.

Kampa Island, situated on the Vltava River between the Lesser Town and the Old Town, is a charming park known for its picturesque setting and cultural attractions. The island features beautiful lawns, tree-lined paths, and stunning views of the river and the Charles Bridge. Kampa Island is also home to several notable landmarks, including the Museum Kampa, which showcases modern and contemporary art, and the iconic waterwheel of the Grand Priory Mill. The island's tranquil atmosphere and scenic beauty make it a popular spot for picnicking, walking, and enjoying the natural surroundings.

The Botanical Garden of the Faculty of Science, Charles University (Botanická zahrada UK) is a hidden gem located in the New Town, near the Vltava River. The garden, established in the late 18th century, features a diverse collection of plants, including a variety of rare and exotic species. The Botanical Garden includes several themed sections, such as an alpine garden, a Japanese garden, and a greenhouse with tropical and subtropical plants. The garden provides a tranquil and educational setting for visitors to explore the world of plants and enjoy the beauty of nature.

By visiting these green spaces, you can gain a deeper appreciation of Prague's natural beauty, cultural heritage, and historical significance, making your visit to this remarkable city truly enriching and memorable.

Hidden Gems

Prague, with its rich tapestry of history and culture, is a city brimming with famous landmarks and well-known attractions. However, beyond the usual tourist spots, the city harbors many hidden gems that offer unique insights and experiences for those willing to explore further. These lesser-known sites provide a more intimate and authentic view of Prague, revealing its multifaceted character and charm.

One of Prague's best-kept secrets is Vyšehrad, a historic fortress situated on a hill overlooking the Vltava River. While not as frequently visited as Prague Castle, Vyšehrad holds immense historical significance and offers breathtaking views of the city. The fortress dates back to the 10th century and includes several notable structures, such as the Basilica of St. Peter and St. Paul, renowned for its stunning Gothic Revival architecture and beautiful frescoes. Vyšehrad Cemetery is the final resting place of many famous Czech figures, including composers Antonín Dvořák and Bedřich Smetana, and writer Karel Čapek. The tranquil gardens and ancient ruins of Vyšehrad provide a peaceful escape and a glimpse into Prague's medieval past.

Another hidden gem is the John Lennon Wall, located in the Lesser Town near the French Embassy. What began as a simple tribute to John Lennon in the 1980s has evolved into a vibrant symbol of peace, love, and artistic expression. The wall is covered in colorful graffiti, murals, and messages inspired by Lennon and the Beatles, reflecting themes of freedom and rebellion. It has become an ever-changing canvas where visitors are encouraged to add their own artwork and messages. The John Lennon Wall is a testament to the enduring power of art and music to inspire change and connect people from around the world.

The Klementinum, a historic complex of buildings near the Charles Bridge, is another treasure waiting to be discovered. Originally a Jesuit college, the Klementinum is home to one of the most beautiful libraries in the world, the Baroque Library Hall. This stunning hall, adorned with ornate frescoes, gilded decorations, and rows of antique globes, houses a vast collection of rare books and manuscripts. Visitors can also climb the Astronomical Tower for a panoramic view of Prague's rooftops and spires. The Klementinum's rich history and architectural splendor make it a must-visit for those interested in Prague's intellectual and cultural heritage.

The New World (Nový Svět) is a charming and picturesque neighborhood located near Prague Castle. This hidden enclave of narrow cobblestone streets and colorful historic houses offers a peaceful retreat from the busy tourist areas. The New World has a bohemian atmosphere, with many of its quaint cottages now home to artists, musicians, and writers. Walking through this area feels like stepping back in time, with its quiet alleys, blooming gardens, and the occasional artist at work. The New World is an ideal place for a leisurely stroll, allowing visitors to soak in the serene ambiance and discover a different side of Prague's history.

Prague's Jewish Quarter, or Josefov, is well-known for its historical significance, but the Jewish Cemetery is a particularly poignant and often overlooked site. Dating back to the 15th century, the Old Jewish Cemetery is one of the oldest and most remarkable Jewish burial grounds in Europe. The cemetery is a maze of weathered tombstones, packed closely together due to the limited space. Many of the stones are intricately carved with Hebrew inscriptions and symbolic motifs. The cemetery's haunting beauty and historical importance make it a powerful reminder of Prague's Jewish heritage and the resilience of its community.

The House of the Black Madonna (Dům U Černé Matky Boží) is a hidden gem for architecture and design enthusiasts. This cubist building, designed by Josef Gočár and completed in 1912, is a rare example of cubist architecture in Prague. The building houses the Museum of Czech Cubism, which showcases a collection of cubist furniture, ceramics, and artworks. The Grand Café Orient, located on the first floor, is a beautifully restored cubist café where visitors can enjoy coffee and pastries in a unique setting. The House of the Black Madonna offers a fascinating glimpse into an important movement in Czech art and architecture.

Another hidden treasure is the Wallenstein Garden (Valdštejnská zahrada), a Baroque garden located next to the Wallenstein Palace in the Lesser Town. This beautifully landscaped garden features ornate statues, manicured hedges, and tranquil ponds. The garden's centerpiece is the impressive sala terrena, a grand open-air pavilion decorated with frescoes and stucco work. The Wallenstein Garden is a peaceful oasis in the heart of the city, providing a serene setting for a leisurely stroll or quiet reflection. The garden is also home to several peacocks, adding to its charm and allure.

The Náplavka Riverbank is a vibrant and trendy area that offers a different perspective on Prague's cultural scene. Located along the Vltava River, Náplavka is known for its lively atmosphere, with a variety of bars, cafes, and food stalls lining the waterfront. On weekends, the area hosts a popular farmers' market, where visitors can sample local produce, artisanal foods, and craft beers. Náplavka is also a hub for cultural events, including live music performances, art exhibitions, and outdoor cinema screenings. The riverbank's dynamic and creative energy makes it a great place to experience contemporary Prague.

For those interested in modern and contemporary art, the DOX Centre for Contemporary Art is a hidden gem worth exploring. Located in the Holešovice district, DOX is one of Prague's leading venues for contemporary art, design, and architecture. The center's innovative exhibitions feature works by both Czech and international artists, covering a wide range of media, including painting, sculpture, photography, and video. DOX also hosts a variety of cultural events, such as lectures, workshops, and performances, making it a vibrant and dynamic cultural hub. The center's striking modernist building, with its distinctive red steel structure, is an architectural landmark in itself.

Prague's Vysočany district, often overlooked by tourists, is home to several hidden gems, including the Pragovka Art District. This former industrial complex has been transformed into a thriving cultural space, with artist studios, galleries, and creative workshops. Pragovka hosts a variety of exhibitions, performances, and events, showcasing contemporary art and culture. The district's gritty, industrial aesthetic provides a unique backdrop for artistic expression and experimentation. Visiting Pragovka offers a glimpse into Prague's vibrant contemporary art scene and the city's ongoing process of cultural renewal.

Finally, the Vrtba Garden (Vrtbovská zahrada) is an exquisite Baroque garden located on the slopes of Petrin Hill in the Lesser Town. Designed in the early 18th century, the garden is renowned for its terraced layout, elaborate statues, and stunning views of Prague. Vrtba Garden features a series of interconnected terraces, each adorned with meticulously maintained flower beds, hedges, and sculptures. The garden's upper terraces offer breathtaking views of the city, including the spires of St. Nicholas Church and Prague

Castle. Vrtba Garden is a hidden gem, providing a tranquil and elegant setting for visitors to enjoy the beauty of Baroque landscape design.

By exploring these lesser-known treasures, you can gain a deeper understanding of Prague's multifaceted charm and uncover the many layers of this remarkable city. Each of these hidden gems contributes to Prague's charm and allure, making it a truly unforgettable destination.

CHAPTER 6

THINGS TO DO IN PRAGUE FOR DIFFERENT TRAVELERS

Solo Travelers

Prague, with its enchanting mix of history, architecture, and culture, is an ideal destination for solo travelers. The city's compact size, excellent public transport, and friendly atmosphere make it easy to explore on your own. Whether you prefer wandering through historic streets, discovering hidden gems, or immersing yourself in the local culture, Prague offers a wealth of activities that can be enjoyed solo.

One of the best ways to begin your exploration of Prague is by taking a leisurely walk across the Charles Bridge (Karlův most). This iconic bridge, lined with 30 statues of saints, connects the Old Town with the Lesser Town. The bridge is a lively spot, often filled with street musicians, artists, and vendors. Early in the morning or late in the evening, when the crowds thin out, is the perfect time to appreciate its beauty and take in the stunning views of the Vltava River and Prague Castle. The experience of walking across the bridge, feeling the cobblestones under your feet, and seeing the city from this vantage point is both serene and captivating.

Once you've crossed the Charles Bridge, make your way to Prague Castle (Pražský hrad). This sprawling complex, which dates back to the 9th century, is one of the largest castles in the world and a UNESCO World Heritage site. Spend a few hours exploring its various attractions, including St. Vitus Cathedral, the Old Royal Palace, and the Golden Lane. The Gothic architecture of St. Vitus Cathedral, with its intricate stained glass windows and towering spires, is awe-inspiring. The Golden Lane, with its charming, colorful houses, provides a glimpse into the lives of the castle's former inhabitants, including artisans and soldiers. As you wander through the castle grounds, you'll also be treated to panoramic views of Prague.

After exploring Prague Castle, head to the Old Town Square (Staroměstské náměstí). This historic square is the heart of Prague and is surrounded by beautiful buildings, including the Old Town Hall and the Church of Our Lady before Týn. The Old Town Hall is home to the famous Astronomical Clock (Orloj), which dates back to 1410 and is one of the oldest working clocks of its kind in the world. Every hour, the clock puts on a show, with a procession of the Twelve Apostles and other figures. Watching this intricate performance is a must-do for any visitor. The square itself is a vibrant place, with cafes, street performers, and markets, making it an excellent spot for people-watching and soaking in the atmosphere.

For a deeper dive into Prague's history, visit the Jewish Quarter (Josefov). This district is rich in history and culture, with several significant sites to explore. The Jewish Museum in Prague, which includes six synagogues, the Old Jewish Cemetery, and the Ceremonial Hall, offers a comprehensive look at the history and culture of Jews in Bohemia and Moravia. The Old Jewish Cemetery, with its ancient, densely packed tombstones, is particularly poignant. Each site within the Jewish Quarter tells a story of resilience and tradition, providing a meaningful and reflective experience.

Solo travelers who enjoy art and architecture should not miss the opportunity to visit the National Gallery in Prague (Národní galerie v Praze). The gallery's collections are housed in several historic buildings across the city, each dedicated to different periods and styles. The Trade Fair Palace (Veletržní palác) is home to modern and contemporary art, featuring works by Picasso, Klimt, and Mucha, as well as Czech artists. The Convent of St. Agnes of Bohemia (Anežský klášter) showcases medieval art, including stunning altarpieces and sculptures. The Kinský Palace (Palác Kinských) displays a collection of Asian art, with artifacts ranging from ancient Chinese ceramics to contemporary Japanese prints. Each visit to these locations is a journey through art history, offering inspiration and insight.

For a unique perspective of Prague, take a walk up Petrin Hill (Petřín). The hill is covered with gardens, orchards, and wooded areas, providing a peaceful escape from the city. At the top of the hill stands the Petrin Lookout Tower, a smaller version of the Eiffel Tower. Climb the 299 steps to the observation deck for a panoramic view of Prague's skyline. On a clear day, you can see for miles, taking in landmarks such as Prague Castle and the Charles Bridge. The hill also features the Mirror Maze, a fun and quirky attraction, and the Rose Garden, which is particularly beautiful in the spring and summer.

Exploring Prague's vibrant neighborhoods is another great way to experience the city as a solo traveler. The Vinohrady district, known for its beautiful Art Nouveau and Neo-Renaissance architecture, is a local favorite. Wander through its tree-lined streets, discover trendy cafes and restaurants, and visit the stunning Church of St. Ludmila on Náměstí Míru (Peace Square). The district is also home to several parks, including Riegrovy Sady, which offers beautiful views of the city and is a popular spot for picnics and sunset watching.

For those interested in contemporary culture, the DOX Centre for Contemporary Art in the Holešovice district is a must-visit. This innovative space features exhibitions by both Czech and international artists, covering a wide range of media, including painting, sculpture, photography, and video. DOX also hosts a variety of cultural events, such as lectures, workshops, and performances, making it a dynamic and engaging venue. The center's modernist architecture, with its striking red steel structure, is an attraction in itself.

Prague's café culture is another aspect that solo travelers can thoroughly enjoy. Spend some time in one of the city's many historic cafes, such as Café Slavia or Café Louvre. These establishments have been meeting places for artists, writers, and intellectuals for decades, and their elegant interiors and rich history create a unique ambiance. Enjoy a coffee and a pastry while reading a book or simply watching the world go by. These cafes are also great places to strike up conversations with locals and fellow travelers.

For an off-the-beaten-path experience, explore the hidden gardens and courtyards scattered throughout Prague. The Vrtba Garden (Vrtbovská zahrada), located in the Lesser Town, is a beautiful Baroque garden with terraced layouts, ornamental statues, and stunning views of the city. The Wallenstein Garden (Valdštejnská zahrada), adjacent to the Wallenstein Palace, features meticulously manicured lawns, fountains, and a tranquil pond. These hidden gems offer a peaceful retreat and a chance to appreciate the city's natural beauty and landscape design.

Prague's nightlife also offers plenty of opportunities for solo travelers. The city is known for its lively bar and club scene, with options to suit all tastes. Join a guided pub crawl to meet fellow travelers and discover some of the best bars in the city. Alternatively, visit one of Prague's renowned jazz clubs, such as Jazz Dock or Reduta Jazz Club, for an evening of live music and great atmosphere. These venues often feature performances by talented local and international musicians, providing an unforgettable experience.

For those who enjoy literature and history, a visit to the Franz Kafka Museum is a must. Located in the Lesser Town, this museum is dedicated to the life and work of one of Prague's most famous literary figures. The exhibits include first editions of Kafka's works, personal letters, and photographs, as well as audiovisual displays that provide deeper insights into Kafka's writing and his connection to Prague. The museum's atmospheric setting, housed in a former brickworks, enhances the experience and immerses visitors in Kafka's world.

Couples

Prague, with its fairy-tale architecture, romantic river views, and charming cobblestone streets, is an ideal destination for couples seeking a romantic getaway. The city offers a multitude of activities and experiences that are perfect for exploring together.

Start your romantic journey in Prague with a leisurely stroll across the Charles Bridge (Karlův most). This iconic bridge, dating back to the 14th century, is lined with statues of saints and offers stunning views of the Vltava River and the city's skyline. Walking hand in hand as the sun rises or sets, when the bridge is less crowded, creates a magical atmosphere. Street musicians, artists, and vendors add to the charm, making it a perfect spot for taking memorable photos.

After crossing the bridge, head to the Old Town Square (Staroměstské náměstí), the heart of Prague's historic center. The square is surrounded by beautiful Gothic, Baroque, and Renaissance buildings, creating a picturesque backdrop. One of the highlights is the Astronomical Clock (Orloj), located on the Old Town Hall. Every hour, the clock puts on a show with a procession of the Twelve Apostles and other figures. Watching this intricate performance together is a must-do for any couple visiting Prague. The square is also home to the Church of Our Lady before Týn and St. Nicholas Church, both of which are worth exploring.

Prague Castle (Pražský hrad) is another must-visit landmark. This vast complex, which dates back to the 9th century, is one of the largest castles in the world. Spend a few hours exploring its various attractions, including St. Vitus Cathedral, the Old Royal Palace, and the Golden Lane. The Gothic architecture of St. Vitus Cathedral, with its intricate stained glass windows and towering spires, is awe-inspiring. The Golden Lane, with its charming, colorful houses, provides a glimpse into the lives of the castle's former inhabitants. As you wander through the castle grounds, you'll also be treated to panoramic views of Prague. Be sure to visit the castle in the evening as well, when it is beautifully illuminated, creating a romantic ambiance.

For a unique perspective of Prague, take a romantic boat ride on the Vltava River. Several companies offer cruises that range from short sightseeing tours to longer dinner cruises. A sunset or evening cruise is particularly romantic, as you can enjoy the city's illuminated landmarks while dining on a delicious meal. The gentle sway of the boat, the shimmering reflections on the water, and the stunning views of the Charles Bridge and Prague Castle create an unforgettable experience.

Petrin Hill (Petřín) is another romantic spot in Prague. Covered with gardens, orchards, and wooded areas, the hill provides a peaceful escape from the bustling city. Take the funicular railway to the top of the hill, where you'll find the Petrin Lookout Tower. This smaller version of the Eiffel Tower offers panoramic views of Prague from its observation deck. Climb the 299 steps to the top, and you'll be rewarded with breathtaking views that stretch for miles. Petrin Hill also features the Mirror Maze, a fun attraction for couples, and the Rose Garden, which is particularly beautiful in the spring and summer. The Hunger Wall, a medieval fortification built during the reign of Charles IV, runs along the hill and adds to its historical significance.

Another romantic activity is exploring the charming neighborhood of Malá Strana (Lesser Town). This area is known for its narrow, winding streets, Baroque palaces, and beautiful gardens. Wander through the picturesque alleys, discovering hidden courtyards and quaint cafes. Visit the Wallenstein Garden (Valdštejnská zahrada), a beautifully landscaped Baroque garden with ornate statues, manicured hedges, and tranquil ponds. The garden's peaceful atmosphere makes it a perfect spot for a romantic stroll. Another highlight of Malá Strana is the John Lennon Wall, covered in colorful graffiti and messages of peace and love. Adding your own message or simply appreciating the art together can be a meaningful experience.

For a taste of Prague's café culture, visit one of the city's historic cafes. Café Slavia, located along the Vltava River, offers stunning views of Prague Castle and the Charles Bridge. This elegant café has been a meeting place for artists, writers, and intellectuals for decades. Enjoy a coffee and a pastry while soaking in the rich history and ambiance. Another iconic café is Café Louvre, which dates back to 1902 and has hosted notable figures such as Franz Kafka and Albert Einstein. The café's Art Nouveau interior and charming atmosphere make it a perfect spot for a romantic coffee break.

A visit to one of Prague's many parks and gardens can also be a delightful experience for couples. The Vrtba Garden (Vrtbovská zahrada) is an exquisite Baroque garden located on the slopes of Petrin Hill. The garden features terraced layouts, ornamental statues, and stunning views of Prague. Wander through the beautifully landscaped terraces, enjoying the tranquil setting and breathtaking views.

Another beautiful garden is the Franciscan Garden (Františkánská zahrada), located near Wenceslas Square. This hidden oasis offers beautifully landscaped flower beds, lawns, and trees, providing a peaceful retreat in the heart of the city.

For couples who enjoy art and culture, a visit to the National Gallery in Prague (Národní galerie v Praze) is a must. The gallery's collections are housed in several historic buildings across the city, each dedicated to different periods and styles. The Trade Fair Palace (Veletržní palác) is home to modern and contemporary art, featuring works by Picasso, Klimt, and Mucha, as well as Czech artists. The Convent of St. Agnes of Bohemia (Anežský klášter) showcases medieval art, including stunning altarpieces and sculptures. The Kinský Palace (Palác Kinských) displays a collection of Asian art, with artifacts ranging from ancient Chinese ceramics to contemporary Japanese prints. Each visit to these locations is a journey through art history, offering inspiration and insight.

Prague's vibrant nightlife also offers plenty of opportunities for couples to enjoy themselves. The city is known for its lively bar and club scene, with options to suit all tastes. For a romantic evening, visit one of Prague's renowned jazz clubs, such as Jazz Dock or Reduta Jazz Club. These venues often feature performances by talented local and international musicians, providing an intimate and atmospheric setting. Alternatively, enjoy a cocktail at one of

Prague's rooftop bars, such as T-Anker or Cloud 9 Sky Bar & Lounge, where you can take in stunning views of the city while sipping on a delicious drink.

For a unique and memorable experience, consider taking a day trip to one of the beautiful castles or towns near Prague. The town of Český Krumlov, a UNESCO World Heritage site, is known for its well-preserved medieval architecture and picturesque setting along the Vltava River. Explore the charming streets, visit the impressive Český Krumlov Castle, and enjoy a meal at one of the town's cozy restaurants. Another great option is Karlštejn Castle, located just a short train ride from Prague. This stunning Gothic castle, built by Charles IV in the 14th century, offers guided tours that provide fascinating insights into its history and architecture. The surrounding countryside also offers beautiful hiking trails, making it a perfect day trip for nature-loving couples.

Families

Prague is an enchanting city that offers a multitude of activities and attractions suitable for family travelers. Its rich history, stunning architecture, and family-friendly atmosphere make it an ideal destination for parents and children alike.

Start your family adventure by exploring the iconic Charles Bridge (Karlův most). This historic bridge, adorned with statues of saints, provides stunning views of the Vltava River and Prague's skyline. Walking across the bridge, you can enjoy the lively atmosphere created by street musicians, artists, and vendors. The early morning or late evening hours are ideal for a less crowded experience. Children will be fascinated by the statues and the opportunity to make a wish by touching the plaque on the statue of St. John of Nepomuk.

A visit to Prague Castle (Pražský hrad) is a must for families. This vast complex, dating back to the 9th century, is one of the largest castles in the world. Spend a few hours exploring its various attractions, including St. Vitus Cathedral, the Old Royal Palace, and the Golden Lane. The Gothic architecture of St. Vitus Cathedral, with its intricate stained glass windows and towering spires, will captivate both adults and children. The Golden Lane, with its charming, colorful houses, offers a glimpse into the lives of the castle's former inhabitants, including artisans and soldiers. The toy museum located within the castle grounds is a hit with children, featuring a collection of toys from different eras and parts of the world.

The Old Town Square (Staroměstské náměstí) is the heart of Prague's historic center and a great place for families to explore. The square is surrounded by beautiful buildings, including the Old Town Hall and the Church of Our Lady before Týn. The Astronomical Clock (Orloj), located on the Old Town Hall, is one of the oldest working clocks of its kind in the world. Every hour, the clock puts on a show with a procession of the Twelve Apostles and other figures. Watching this intricate performance is a must-do for any family visiting Prague. The square is also home to various street performers, making it an entertaining spot for children.

For a unique perspective of Prague, take a boat ride on the Vltava River. Several companies offer river cruises that range from short sightseeing tours to longer dinner cruises. A daytime cruise is particularly enjoyable for families, as you can see the city's landmarks from the water and enjoy the gentle sway of the boat. Some cruises offer live commentary, providing interesting facts and stories about the sights you pass. The river cruise is a relaxing way to see the city and is sure to be a highlight of your trip.

Petrin Hill (Petřín) is another great spot for families. Covered with gardens, orchards, and wooded areas, the hill provides a peaceful escape from the bustling city. Take the funicular railway to the top of the hill, where you'll find the Petrin Lookout Tower. This smaller version of the Eiffel Tower offers panoramic views of Prague from its observation deck. Climbing the 299 steps to the top is an adventure in itself and provides a sense of accomplishment for children. Petrin Hill also features the Mirror Maze, a fun and quirky attraction that will delight kids of all ages. The Rose Garden on Petrin Hill is particularly beautiful in the spring and summer, with its vibrant blooms and fragrant scents.

The Prague Zoo (Zoo Praha) is one of the best zoos in the world and a fantastic destination for families. Located in the Troja district, the zoo is home to a wide variety of animals, including elephants, giraffes, lions, and penguins. The zoo's spacious enclosures and naturalistic habitats provide excellent conditions for the animals and an engaging experience for visitors. Highlights of the zoo include the African Savannah, the Indonesian Jungle, and the Bororo Reserve. The zoo also offers several play areas, picnic spots, and interactive exhibits, making it a fun and educational outing for children.

A visit to the National Technical Museum (Národní technické muzeum) is a great way to engage children with science and technology. Located near Letná Park, the museum features a wide range of exhibits on topics such as transportation, astronomy, photography, and architecture. Children will be fascinated by the collection of vintage cars, airplanes, and trains, as well as the interactive displays and hands-on activities. The museum's planetarium and observatory offer additional educational experiences, providing a closer look at the wonders of the universe.

The Letná Park (Letenské sady) is another excellent spot for families to enjoy outdoor activities. This expansive park, located on Letná Hill, offers wide, tree-lined avenues perfect for walking, cycling, or rollerblading. The park provides stunning views of the Vltava River and Prague's skyline, making it a great place for a picnic or a leisurely stroll. Letná

Park is also home to several playgrounds and sports facilities, providing plenty of opportunities for children to run, play, and explore.

For a taste of Prague's history and culture, visit the Vyšehrad Fortress. This historic site, located on a hill overlooking the Vltava River, includes several notable structures, such as the Basilica of St. Peter and St. Paul and the Vyšehrad Cemetery. The fortress grounds feature parkland, walking paths, and ruins of medieval structures, providing a serene and picturesque setting for a family outing. The park's elevated position offers breathtaking views of the city and the river, making it a popular spot for picnicking and leisurely strolls. The children will enjoy exploring the ancient ruins and learning about the history of this significant site.

For a fun and interactive experience, visit the Prague Toy Museum (Muzeum hraček). Located within the Prague Castle complex, the museum features a vast collection of toys from different eras and parts of the world. The exhibits include dolls, teddy bears, model trains, and tin soldiers, as well as modern toys such as LEGO and Barbie. The museum's playful atmosphere and nostalgic displays will captivate both children and adults, making it a delightful stop during your visit to the castle.

A visit to the Museum of Senses is a must for families seeking a unique and interactive experience. Located in the heart of Prague, this museum features a variety of exhibits and installations that challenge your perception and stimulate your senses. From optical illusions and mind-bending puzzles to tactile experiences and sensory rooms, the Museum of Senses offers a fun and educational outing for visitors of all ages. The hands-on exhibits encourage exploration and curiosity, making it an engaging experience for children.

Another great family activity is visiting the Kampa Museum, located on Kampa Island in the Lesser Town. The museum is dedicated to modern and contemporary art and features works by Central European artists. The island itself is a picturesque park with beautiful lawns, tree-lined paths, and stunning views of the Charles Bridge and the Vltava River. The island's tranquil atmosphere and scenic beauty make it a perfect spot for a family picnic or a leisurely walk. The museum's outdoor sculpture garden, featuring works by renowned artists, adds an extra layer of interest and creativity to your visit.

For families interested in medieval history, a day trip to the town of Kutná Hora is highly recommended. Located about an hour's drive from Prague, Kutná Hora is home to several UNESCO World Heritage sites, including the Sedlec Ossuary (Bone Church) and the Church of St. Barbara. The Sedlec Ossuary is a small chapel decorated with the bones of approximately 40,000 people, arranged in intricate designs and patterns. While it may sound macabre, the ossuary is a fascinating and unique site that provides insight into medieval practices and beliefs. The Church of St. Barbara, with its stunning Gothic architecture and beautifully decorated interior, is another highlight of Kutná Hora. The town's charming streets, historical sites, and family-friendly atmosphere make it a perfect day trip from Prague.

Adventure Seekers

Prague, with its rich history, stunning architecture, and vibrant cultural scene, also offers a wide range of activities for adventure seekers. Whether you enjoy exploring the great outdoors, seeking thrills, or discovering hidden gems, Prague provides ample opportunities to satisfy your adventurous spirit.

Start your adventure in Prague with a visit to Vyšehrad, an ancient fortress that offers a mix of history, stunning views, and outdoor exploration. Perched on a hill overlooking the Vltava River, Vyšehrad is believed to date back to the 10th century. The fortress includes several historical buildings, such as the Basilica of St. Peter and St. Paul, with its striking twin spires, and the Vyšehrad Cemetery, the final resting place of many notable Czech figures. The fortress grounds feature expansive parkland, walking paths, and ancient ruins, providing a perfect setting for exploration and discovery. The elevated position of Vyšehrad offers breathtaking panoramic views of Prague, making it an excellent spot for photography enthusiasts.

For those seeking a unique perspective of Prague, a hot air balloon ride is an unforgettable experience. Several companies offer hot air balloon flights over the picturesque countryside surrounding Prague. As you gently float above the landscape, you'll be treated to stunning views of rolling hills, charming villages, and historic castles. The experience of drifting silently through the sky, watching the sunrise or sunset, and seeing the world from above is truly magical and provides a sense of adventure and wonder.

Exploring the underground world of Prague is another thrilling adventure. The city is home to several historical tunnels, catacombs, and cellars that offer a glimpse into its hidden past. One such place is the Prague Underground Tour, which takes you beneath the Old Town to explore a labyrinth of ancient tunnels and cellars. These underground passages were once used for storage, shelter, and defense, and they provide a fascinating insight into Prague's history. The tour is led by knowledgeable guides who share intriguing stories and facts about the city's underground secrets.

For adrenaline junkies, bungee jumping off the Zvikov Bridge is an experience not to be missed. Located about an hour's drive from Prague, the Zvikov Bridge offers a thrilling bungee jumping experience with stunning views of the Vltava River and the surrounding countryside. The jump is approximately 50 meters high, providing an exhilarating free fall and a rush of adrenaline. The bungee jumping company ensures strict safety measures and professional guidance, making it a safe and unforgettable adventure.

Rock climbing enthusiasts will find plenty of opportunities to challenge themselves in and around Prague. The Divoká Šárka Nature Reserve, located on the outskirts of the city, is a popular spot for rock climbing. The reserve features impressive rocky cliffs, lush forests, and scenic trails, making it an ideal destination for outdoor activities. The climbing routes in Divoká Šárka cater to various skill levels, from beginners to experienced climbers. The reserve also offers hiking and cycling trails, providing a diverse range of adventures in a beautiful natural setting.

For water sports enthusiasts, kayaking and paddleboarding on the Vltava River offer an exciting way to see Prague from a different perspective. Several rental companies provide kayaks and paddleboards, along with guided tours and lessons for beginners. Paddling along the river, you'll have the opportunity to see some of Prague's most famous landmarks, such as the Charles Bridge and Prague Castle, from the water. The calm waters of the Vltava River make it a suitable activity for all skill levels, and the experience of gliding past the city's stunning architecture is truly memorable.

Cycling is another great way to explore Prague and its surrounding areas. The city offers a network of cycling paths and routes that cater to different skill levels and preferences. One popular route is the Prague-Vienna Greenways, a long-distance cycling trail that connects Prague with Vienna, passing through picturesque countryside, charming towns, and historic sites. While the entire route is quite extensive, you can choose to cycle shorter segments that suit your schedule and fitness level. Cycling through Prague's beautiful parks, along the Vltava River, and through the scenic countryside provides an adventurous and immersive way to experience the region.

For a unique and adventurous experience, try an escape room in Prague. Escape rooms are interactive, puzzle-solving games where participants are locked in a themed room and must work together to find clues, solve puzzles, and escape within a set time limit. Prague offers a variety of escape rooms with different themes and difficulty levels, catering to both beginners and experienced players. Whether you're navigating a haunted house, solving a detective mystery, or escaping from a prison cell, the thrill and challenge of an escape room make for an exciting and memorable adventure.

If you're interested in history and archaeology, a visit to the Sedlec Ossuary, also known as the Bone Church, is a fascinating and eerie experience. Located in Kutná Hora, about an hour's drive from Prague, the Sedlec Ossuary is a small chapel decorated with the bones of approximately 40,000 people. The bones are arranged in intricate designs and patterns, creating chandeliers, coats of arms, and other macabre decorations. The ossuary provides a unique and thought-provoking glimpse into medieval practices and beliefs, making it a must-visit for adventure seekers with an interest in history.

Exploring the natural beauty of the Bohemian Paradise (Český ráj) is another fantastic adventure for nature lovers. This protected landscape area, located about an hour and a half from Prague, is known for its stunning rock formations, lush forests, and picturesque castles. The region offers a variety of outdoor activities, including hiking, rock climbing, and cycling. One of the highlights is the Prachov Rocks, a labyrinth of towering sandstone formations that provide breathtaking views and challenging climbing routes. The Bohemian Paradise also features several historic castles, such as Trosky Castle and Kost Castle, adding a touch of history and mystery to your adventure.

For an underwater adventure, visit the Aquapalace Prague, one of the largest water parks in Central Europe. Located on the outskirts of the city, Aquapalace offers a wide range of water attractions, including slides, wave pools, and a lazy river. The park also features a large indoor diving center, where visitors can try scuba diving in a controlled environment. The diving center offers lessons for beginners, as well as opportunities for experienced divers to explore underwater caves and wrecks. Aquapalace Prague provides a fun and adventurous experience for visitors of all ages.

Culture Enthusiasts

Prague, with its rich history, stunning architecture, and vibrant cultural scene, is a treasure trove for culture enthusiasts. The city offers a plethora of activities and experiences that provide deep insights into its artistic, historical, and cultural heritage.

Start your cultural exploration of Prague with a visit to the Prague Castle (Pražský hrad). This sprawling complex, dating back to the 9th century, is a UNESCO World Heritage site and one of the largest castles in the world. The castle is home to several significant historical buildings, including the magnificent St. Vitus Cathedral, the Old Royal Palace, and the Golden Lane. St. Vitus Cathedral, with its stunning Gothic architecture, intricate stained glass windows, and towering spires, is a masterpiece of medieval craftsmanship. The Old Royal Palace, once the seat of Bohemian kings, offers a glimpse into the history of Czech royalty. The Golden Lane, with its charming, colorful houses, was once home to the castle's goldsmiths and other artisans. Each of these sites provides a unique perspective on Prague's rich history and cultural heritage.

The Old Town Square (Staroměstské náměstí) is another must-visit destination for culture enthusiasts. This historic square is surrounded by beautiful Gothic, Baroque, and Renaissance buildings, creating a picturesque backdrop. The Old Town Hall, with its famous Astronomical Clock (Orloj), is one of the square's highlights. The clock, installed in 1410, is one of the oldest working astronomical clocks in the world. Every hour, the clock puts on a show, featuring a procession of the Twelve Apostles and other figures. The intricate performance is a marvel of medieval engineering and artistry. The square is also home to the Church of Our Lady before Týn and the Baroque-style St. Nicholas Church, both of which are worth exploring for their architectural beauty and historical significance.

The Jewish Quarter (Josefov) is another culturally rich area in Prague. This district, named after Emperor Joseph II, who implemented reforms that improved the living conditions of Jews in the late 18th century, is home to several important landmarks. The Jewish Museum in Prague, which includes six synagogues, the Old Jewish Cemetery, and the Ceremonial Hall, offers a comprehensive look at the history and culture of the Jewish community in Prague and Bohemia. The Spanish Synagogue, with its stunning Moorish Revival interior, is particularly noteworthy. The Old Jewish Cemetery, dating back to the 15th century, is one of the oldest Jewish burial sites in Europe and provides a poignant insight into the Jewish community's history.

For art enthusiasts, a visit to the National Gallery in Prague (Národní galerie v Praze) is a must. The gallery's extensive collections are housed in several historic buildings across the city, each dedicated to different periods and styles. The Trade Fair Palace (Veletržní palác) is home to the gallery's modern and contemporary art collections, featuring works by renowned artists such as Picasso, Klimt, and Mucha, as well as prominent Czech artists. The Convent of St. Agnes of Bohemia (Anežský klášter) showcases the gallery's medieval art collection, including stunning altarpieces and sculptures. The Kinský Palace (Palác Kinských) houses the gallery's collection of Asian art, with exhibits ranging from ancient Chinese ceramics to contemporary Japanese prints. Each visit to these locations is a journey through art history, offering inspiration and insight into the cultural heritage of Prague.

The Mucha Museum is another essential stop for art lovers. Dedicated to the life and work of Alphonse Mucha, one of the most famous Czech artists and a key figure in the Art Nouveau movement, the museum is located in the Baroque Kaunický Palace. The museum features an extensive collection of Mucha's posters, paintings, photographs, and personal memorabilia. Highlights include Mucha's iconic posters for Sarah Bernhardt's theatrical productions and his monumental series of paintings, The Slav Epic, which depicts the history of the Slavic people. The museum provides a comprehensive overview of Mucha's artistic career and his contributions to the Art Nouveau style.

For those interested in architecture, the House of the Black Madonna (Dům U Černé Matky Boží) is a hidden gem. This cubist building, designed by Josef Gočár and completed in 1912, is a rare example of cubist architecture in Prague. The building houses the Museum of Czech Cubism, which showcases a collection of cubist furniture, ceramics, and artworks. The Grand Café Orient, located on the first floor, is a beautifully restored cubist café where visitors can enjoy coffee and pastries in a unique setting. The House of the Black Madonna offers a fascinating glimpse into an important movement in Czech art and architecture.

The Klementinum, a historic complex of buildings near the Charles Bridge, is another treasure waiting to be discovered. Originally a Jesuit college, the Klementinum is home to one of the most beautiful libraries in the world, the Baroque Library Hall. This stunning hall, adorned with ornate frescoes, gilded decorations, and rows of antique globes, houses a vast collection of rare books and manuscripts. Visitors can also climb the Astronomical Tower for a panoramic view of Prague's rooftops and spires. The Klementinum's rich history and architectural splendor make it a must-visit for those interested in Prague's intellectual and cultural heritage.

The Wallenstein Garden (Valdštejnská zahrada) is a beautifully landscaped Baroque garden located next to the Wallenstein Palace in the Lesser Town. Designed in the early 17th century, the garden features meticulously manicured lawns, ornamental flower beds, and a series of elegant statues and fountains. One of the garden's highlights is the impressive sala terrena, a grand open-air pavilion decorated with frescoes and stucco work. The Wallenstein

Garden provides a peaceful retreat in the heart of the city, offering a serene and picturesque setting for relaxation and contemplation.

For music lovers, a visit to the Estates Theatre (Stavovské divadlo) is a must. This historic theatre, located in the Old Town, is one of the oldest opera houses in Europe. It is renowned for its association with Wolfgang Amadeus Mozart, who conducted the premiere of his opera Don Giovanni here in 1787. The theatre's beautifully preserved interior and excellent acoustics make it a perfect venue for experiencing classical music, opera, and ballet performances. Attending a performance at the Estates Theatre is a cultural highlight that should not be missed.

The Municipal House (Obecní dům) is another cultural landmark that offers a rich blend of history, architecture, and the arts. This stunning Art Nouveau building, located near the Powder Tower, is a masterpiece of early 20th-century design. The Municipal House hosts a variety of cultural events, including concerts, exhibitions, and theatre performances. The building's interior is adorned with intricate mosaics, stained glass, and sculptures, making it a visual feast for visitors. The Smetana Hall, the main concert hall, is renowned for its excellent acoustics and hosts performances by the Prague Symphony Orchestra and other prominent ensembles.

For those interested in contemporary culture, the DOX Centre for Contemporary Art is a must-visit. Located in the Holešovice district, DOX is one of Prague's leading venues for contemporary art, design, and architecture. The center's innovative exhibitions feature works by both Czech and international artists, covering a wide range of media, including painting, sculpture, photography, and video. DOX also hosts a variety of cultural events, such as lectures, workshops, and performances, making it a vibrant and dynamic cultural hub. The center's striking modernist building, with its distinctive red steel structure, is an architectural landmark in itself.

The National Museum (Národní muzeum) is another essential destination for culture enthusiasts. Founded in 1818, the museum is housed in a grand Neo-Renaissance building located at the top of Wenceslas Square. The National Museum's extensive collection spans natural history, anthropology, archaeology, art, and music. The museum's exhibits include fossils, minerals, and taxidermy specimens, as well as artifacts from prehistoric times to the present day. The museum also features a vast collection of Czech and Slovak historical documents, providing valuable insights into the country's history. The recently renovated building itself is a marvel, with its grand staircase, intricate ceiling frescoes, and impressive dome offering breathtaking views of the city.

A visit to the Museum of Decorative Arts (Uměleckoprůmyslové museum) is another enriching experience for culture enthusiasts. The museum offers an extensive collection of decorative and applied arts, including glass, ceramics, textiles, furniture, and fashion. The exhibits showcase the development of decorative arts from the Renaissance to the present day, with a particular emphasis on Czech and Central European design. The museum's glass collection is especially noteworthy, featuring exquisite examples of Bohemian glass and contemporary glass art. The museum also houses a comprehensive collection of photography, including works by Czech photographers such as Josef Sudek and František Drtikol.

Prague's café culture is another aspect that culture enthusiasts can thoroughly enjoy. Spend some time in one of the city's historic cafes, such as Café Slavia or Café Louvre. These establishments have been meeting places for artists, writers, and intellectuals for decades, and their elegant interiors and rich history create a unique ambiance. Enjoy a coffee and a pastry while reading a book or simply watching the world go by. These cafes are also great places to strike up conversations with locals and fellow travelers.

For literature enthusiasts, a visit to the Franz Kafka Museum is a must. Located in the Lesser Town, this museum is dedicated to the life and work of one of Prague's most famous literary figures. The museum's exhibits include first editions of Kafka's works, personal letters, and photographs, as well as audiovisual displays that provide a deeper understanding of Kafka's writing and his connection to Prague. The museum's atmospheric setting, housed in a former brickworks, enhances the experience and immerses visitors in Kafka's world.

CHAPTER 7

DINING IN PRAGUE

Traditional Czech Cuisine

Traditional Czech cuisine is a rich tapestry of flavors and ingredients that reflect the country's agricultural heritage and the influence of neighboring cultures. It is hearty and comforting, making use of meats, root vegetables, and dairy products to create dishes that are both satisfying and flavorful.

One of the staples of Czech cuisine is bread, particularly a type of bread known as "chléb." This dark, dense rye bread is often served with meals and is an essential part of the Czech diet. It is commonly enjoyed with butter, cheese, or cold cuts and is also used to make open-faced sandwiches called "chlebíčky." These sandwiches are typically topped with a variety of ingredients, such as ham, salami, hard-boiled eggs, pickles, and spreads, and are a popular snack or appetizer.

Soups play a crucial role in Czech cuisine and are often enjoyed as a starter for both lunch and dinner. One of the most traditional soups is "česnečka," a garlic soup made with broth, potatoes, and plenty of garlic, often garnished with croutons and cheese. Another popular soup is "kulajda," a creamy soup made with mushrooms, potatoes, dill, and a touch of vinegar, usually served with a poached egg. "Bramboračka" is another classic, a hearty potato soup filled with root vegetables, mushrooms, and spices, perfect for cold weather.

Main dishes in Czech cuisine are typically meat-based, with pork being the most commonly consumed meat. "Vepřo knedlo zelo" is perhaps the most iconic Czech dish, consisting of roast pork served with sauerkraut and dumplings. The dumplings, known as "knedlíky," are made from flour, eggs, and milk, and are either boiled or steamed. They can be sliced and served as a side dish or used as a base for other dishes.

Another beloved meat dish is "svíčková na smetaně," which features marinated beef sirloin served with a creamy vegetable sauce made from carrots, parsley root, celery, and onions. The dish is often garnished with a slice of lemon, a dollop of cranberry sauce, and a generous serving of dumplings. The combination of tender beef, rich sauce, and soft dumplings makes svíčková a favorite for special occasions and family gatherings.

For those who enjoy poultry, "pečená kachna" or roast duck is a popular choice. The duck is typically seasoned with caraway seeds, marjoram, and garlic, then slow-roasted until the skin is crispy and the meat is tender. It is usually served with red cabbage and potato dumplings. Another traditional poultry dish is "kuře na paprice," chicken in paprika sauce, which features chicken pieces cooked in a creamy, paprika-infused sauce and served with rice or dumplings.

Fish also has a place in Czech cuisine, particularly freshwater fish such as carp and trout. Carp is especially significant during Christmas, when it is traditionally served as the main course for the Christmas Eve dinner. The fish is often breaded and fried, then served with potato salad. Trout, on the other hand, is commonly grilled or baked with herbs and served with lemon and potatoes.

Czech cuisine also includes a variety of hearty stews. "Guláš," a dish influenced by Hungarian cuisine, is a meat stew made with beef, onions, paprika, and other spices. It is typically served with bread dumplings or slices of chléb. Another popular stew is "rajská omáčka," a tomato-based sauce served with beef, pork, or meatballs and accompanied by rice or dumplings. The sweet and tangy flavor of the tomato sauce makes it a favorite among both adults and children.

For those with a sweet tooth, Czech desserts offer a delightful array of treats. "Koláče" are traditional pastries made from sweet yeast dough and filled with various ingredients such as poppy seeds, fruit preserves, or sweetened farmer's cheese. These pastries are often enjoyed with a cup of coffee or tea. Another popular dessert is "trdelník," a cylindrical pastry made from rolled dough that is wrapped around a stick, then grilled and coated with sugar and walnuts. While trdelník is often associated with street fairs and Christmas markets, it is enjoyed year-round.

"Dukátové buchtičky" are sweet yeast rolls served with a creamy vanilla sauce. This dessert is a favorite among children and is often enjoyed as a treat after lunch. Another traditional sweet dish is "palačinky," thin pancakes similar to crepes, which can be filled with a variety of sweet fillings such as jam, fruit, whipped cream, or chocolate sauce. These are typically enjoyed as a dessert or a special breakfast treat.

In addition to these traditional dishes, Czech cuisine also includes a variety of beverages that complement the food. Beer, or "pivo," holds a special place in Czech culture and is considered the national drink. The Czech Republic has the highest beer consumption per capita in the world, and the country is known for its high-quality lagers. Popular Czech beer brands include Pilsner Urquell, Budweiser Budvar, and Staropramen. Beer is often enjoyed with meals or in social settings at pubs, known as "hospody."

For those who prefer non-alcoholic beverages, "kofola" is a popular Czech soft drink similar to cola but with a distinct herbal flavor. It was created during the communist era as a local alternative to Western cola brands and remains a favorite among Czechs. Another traditional beverage is "svařák," a type of mulled wine made with red wine, spices, and sugar, typically enjoyed during the winter months at Christmas markets and festive gatherings.

Czech cuisine also places a strong emphasis on seasonal and locally sourced ingredients. In the spring, dishes often feature fresh herbs, young vegetables, and wild mushrooms. Summer brings an abundance of fruits, which are used in a variety of desserts and preserves. Autumn is the season for game meats, root vegetables, and hearty stews, while winter calls for warming soups, roasted meats, and traditional Christmas dishes.

International Dining

Prague is not only renowned for its stunning architecture and rich history but also for its diverse and vibrant dining scene. The city offers a plethora of international dining options that cater to a wide range of tastes and preferences. From traditional Czech fare to exotic flavors from around the globe, Prague's culinary landscape is a testament to its cosmopolitan nature and its embrace of global cuisine.

One of the highlights of Prague's international dining scene is its array of Italian restaurants. Italian cuisine is immensely popular in Prague, and you will find numerous eateries offering authentic Italian dishes made with high-quality ingredients. La Finestra in Cucina is a notable example, known for its dedication to using fresh, seasonal ingredients. The restaurant offers a wide range of classic Italian dishes, from handmade pasta to perfectly cooked risotto and succulent meat dishes. Their extensive wine list features a variety of Italian wines that complement the food beautifully.

Another excellent Italian dining option is Aromi, a restaurant that specializes in seafood and traditional Italian recipes. The elegant setting and attentive service make it an ideal spot for a romantic dinner or a special occasion. Dishes like octopus carpaccio, black ink risotto, and homemade ravioli are crafted with care and precision, delivering an authentic taste of Italy in the heart of Prague.

For those who crave Asian flavors, Prague boasts a variety of restaurants that offer an array of dishes from across the continent. SaSaZu is one of the city's most renowned Asian fusion restaurants, offering a menu that blends Thai, Vietnamese, Japanese, and Indonesian cuisines. The vibrant and stylish interior sets the stage for a culinary journey through Asia, with dishes like beef rendang, sushi rolls, and Thai curry that are both visually appealing and delicious.

Yamato, a Japanese restaurant, is another standout in Prague's dining scene. Known for its high-quality sushi and sashimi, Yamato offers a traditional Japanese dining experience. The chefs use fresh, high-quality ingredients to create beautifully presented dishes that are a feast for the senses. In addition to sushi, the menu includes a variety of other Japanese favorites such as tempura, ramen, and yakitori.

For fans of Indian cuisine, the city offers several excellent options. Indian by Nature is a popular restaurant that serves a wide range of traditional Indian dishes, from flavorful curries to tandoori specialties. The warm and inviting atmosphere, combined with the rich and aromatic flavors of the food, makes it a favorite among both locals and tourists. Another great choice is K The Two Brothers, which offers a diverse menu featuring dishes from various regions of India. The restaurant's modern and stylish decor provides a comfortable setting to enjoy dishes like butter chicken, lamb rogan josh, and vegetarian thali.

Middle Eastern cuisine is also well-represented in Prague. Restaurace Mangal offers an authentic taste of Turkish cuisine, with dishes like kebabs, mezes, and baklava. The restaurant's cozy and welcoming atmosphere, along with its flavorful and aromatic dishes, make it a great place to enjoy a meal with family or friends. Another excellent option is Marthy's Kitchen, a Lebanese restaurant known for its delicious hummus, falafel, and shawarma. The vibrant and colorful interior adds to the overall dining experience, making it a popular spot for those seeking Middle Eastern flavors.

For a taste of South America, La Casa Argentina is a top choice in Prague. This lively and colorful restaurant offers a menu filled with traditional Argentinean dishes, such as empanadas, grilled meats, and chimichurri sauce. The restaurant's energetic atmosphere, complete with live music and tango performances, transports diners to the heart of Argentina. The quality of the food and the vibrant ambiance make La Casa Argentina a must-visit for those craving South American cuisine.

French cuisine is also well-represented in Prague, with several restaurants offering classic French dishes and fine dining experiences. Café Savoy is a charming brasserie that serves traditional French and Czech cuisine in an elegant setting. The menu features dishes like coq au vin, escargot, and crème brûlée, all prepared with a focus on quality and authenticity. The beautiful interior, with its high ceilings and ornate decor, adds to the overall dining experience.

Another excellent French dining option is La Gare, a stylish restaurant that offers a wide range of French dishes, from hearty stews to delicate pastries. The restaurant's extensive wine list features a selection of French wines that pair perfectly with the food. The combination of delicious cuisine, attentive service, and elegant ambiance makes La Gare a popular choice for those seeking a taste of France in Prague.

Prague also offers a variety of international street food options, perfect for those who want to enjoy a quick and flavorful meal on the go. The city's street food scene has grown significantly in recent years, with food trucks and market stalls offering a diverse range of cuisines. Manifesto Market, an innovative food market located in the city center, is a prime example. The market features a variety of food stalls offering everything from gourmet burgers and tacos to sushi and vegan dishes. The lively atmosphere, combined with the wide range of food options, makes Manifesto Market a popular destination for both locals and visitors.

In addition to these diverse dining options, Prague also hosts several food festivals throughout the year, celebrating the city's culinary diversity. The Prague Food Festival, held annually in the spring, showcases a wide range of dishes from some of the city's top restaurants. Visitors can sample a variety of cuisines, from traditional Czech fare to international delicacies, all in one place. The festival also features cooking demonstrations, workshops, and live entertainment, making it a fun and educational experience for food lovers.

Another popular event is the Vietnamese Street Food Festival, which celebrates the vibrant flavors of Vietnamese cuisine. The festival features a variety of food stalls offering dishes like pho, banh mi, and spring rolls, as well as traditional Vietnamese drinks and desserts. The lively atmosphere, complete with cultural performances and activities, makes it a great way to experience the rich culinary heritage of Vietnam.

For those interested in exploring Prague's culinary scene further, food tours are a great option. Several companies offer guided food tours that take visitors to some of the city's best restaurants, cafes, and markets. These tours provide an opportunity to sample a variety of dishes, learn about the history and culture of the cuisine, and meet the chefs and artisans behind the food. Whether you're interested in traditional Czech cuisine or international flavors, a food tour is a fantastic way to discover the diverse and vibrant dining scene in Prague.

CHAPTER 8

NIGHTLIFE IN PRAGUE

Bars and Pubs

Prague is renowned for its rich cultural history, stunning architecture, and vibrant nightlife. The city offers a wide variety of bars and pubs that cater to all tastes, making it a haven for those who enjoy a good drink and a lively atmosphere. From traditional Czech beer halls to modern cocktail bars, Prague's nightlife is as diverse as it is exciting.

The Czech Republic is famous for its beer, and Prague is no exception. The city boasts a number of historic beer halls and pubs that offer an authentic taste of Czech beer culture. One of the most famous beer halls is U Fleků, which has been brewing its own beer since 1499. This iconic pub is known for its dark lager, which is served in large, communal beer halls where visitors can enjoy live music and traditional Czech dishes. The atmosphere is lively and convivial, making it a great place to experience the local culture and meet new people.

Another must-visit for beer enthusiasts is Pivovarský Dům, a brewery pub that offers a wide range of house-brewed beers. The pub is known for its innovative flavors, including banana beer, coffee beer, and nettle beer. The cozy and welcoming atmosphere, combined with the unique beer offerings, makes Pivovarský Dům a popular spot for both locals and tourists. The pub also serves traditional Czech cuisine, providing a well-rounded dining and drinking experience.

For those who prefer a more modern take on beer, Lokál is a chain of pubs that has become synonymous with high-quality, fresh beer. Each Lokál pub serves unpasteurized Pilsner Urquell straight from the tanks, ensuring the freshest possible taste. The minimalist decor and relaxed atmosphere create a comfortable setting for enjoying a few pints with friends. Lokál also prides itself on serving traditional Czech dishes made from locally sourced ingredients, making it a great place to sample authentic Czech cuisine.

Prague is also home to a number of craft beer bars that offer a diverse selection of local and international brews. BeerGeek Bar is a standout in this category, with a rotating selection of over 30 beers on tap. The bar features a mix of Czech and international craft beers, ensuring there is something for every palate. The knowledgeable staff are always on hand to offer recommendations and guide you through the extensive beer menu. The bar's lively and informal atmosphere makes it a popular spot for beer enthusiasts and casual drinkers alike.

If you're looking for a more upscale experience, Prague's cocktail bars offer a sophisticated and stylish alternative to the traditional beer halls. Hemingway Bar is one of the city's most renowned cocktail bars, known for its creative and expertly crafted drinks. The bar is inspired by the life and works of Ernest Hemingway, and the menu features a range of classic and signature cocktails. The intimate and elegant setting, combined with the skilled bartenders, make Hemingway Bar a must-visit for cocktail aficionados.

Another excellent cocktail bar is Black Angel's Bar, located in the basement of the Hotel U Prince. This speakeasy-style bar offers a unique and atmospheric setting, with its vaulted ceilings and candlelit tables. The bartenders are known for their expertise and creativity, and the menu features a mix of classic cocktails and original creations. The bar's location in the heart of Prague's Old Town adds to its charm and appeal.

For a more laid-back and eclectic vibe, The Anonymous Bar offers a unique drinking experience inspired by the hacktivist group Anonymous. The bar's decor features masks and other symbols associated with the group, creating a mysterious and intriguing atmosphere. The cocktail menu is equally creative, with drinks served in unconventional vessels and garnished with unusual ingredients. The Anonymous Bar's innovative approach to mixology and its distinctive setting make it a standout in Prague's cocktail scene.

Prague also offers a variety of wine bars for those who prefer a glass of wine over beer or cocktails. Vinograf is a popular wine bar with several locations throughout the city. The bar offers an extensive selection of Czech and international wines, with a focus on quality and variety. The knowledgeable staff are always on hand to offer recommendations and guide you through the wine list. The relaxed and elegant setting makes Vinograf a great place to unwind and enjoy a glass of wine.

For a more unique wine experience, Bokovka is a hidden gem located in a charming courtyard in the heart of Prague. The bar's rustic and intimate setting, combined with its carefully curated selection of wines, creates a warm and welcoming atmosphere. Bokovka specializes in natural and biodynamic wines, offering a unique and sustainable approach to wine drinking. The bar also serves a selection of cheese and charcuterie, making it a great spot for a relaxed evening with friends.

In addition to these established bars and pubs, Prague is also home to a number of unique and quirky drinking spots. The Pub, for example, is a chain of self-service beer bars where customers can pour their own beer from taps located at their tables. The bars also feature a digital scoreboard that tracks how much beer each table has consumed, adding a fun and competitive element to the drinking experience.

Another unique spot is Cross Club, a multi-level venue that combines a bar, nightclub, and cultural space. The club's eclectic decor, featuring recycled materials and industrial elements, creates a visually striking and immersive environment. Cross Club hosts a variety of events, including live music, DJ sets, and art exhibitions, making it a vibrant and dynamic spot for a night out.

For those interested in exploring Prague's nightlife further, several companies offer guided pub crawls that take visitors to some of the city's best bars and pubs. These tours provide an opportunity to sample a variety of drinks, meet new people, and experience Prague's nightlife in a fun and social setting. Whether you're interested in traditional Czech beer halls, modern cocktail bars, or unique and quirky spots, a pub crawl is a great way to discover the diverse and vibrant drinking scene in Prague.

Nightclubs and Live Music Venues

Prague, a city renowned for its historical charm and architectural beauty, also boasts a vibrant nightlife scene. This includes an array of nightclubs and live music venues that cater to diverse musical tastes and provide unforgettable experiences. Whether you are looking to dance the night away in a high-energy club or enjoy an intimate live music performance, Prague has something for every night owl.

One of the most iconic nightclubs in Prague is Karlovy Lázně, reputed to be the largest nightclub in Central Europe. This multi-level club, located near the Charles Bridge, spans five floors, each with its own distinct theme and musical style. The floors include everything from dance and techno to hip-hop and oldies, ensuring there is something for everyone. The historical building, which dates back to the 14th century, adds to the club's unique atmosphere. The club's high-energy environment, diverse music, and impressive light shows make it a must-visit for those looking to experience Prague's nightlife at its most vibrant.

For those seeking a more upscale and exclusive nightclub experience, Duplex is an excellent choice. Located on Wenceslas Square, this rooftop club offers stunning views of the city, particularly at night. Duplex combines a stylish interior with a dynamic party atmosphere, featuring top DJs, state-of-the-art sound and lighting systems, and a spacious dance floor. The club also includes a restaurant and lounge area, providing a more relaxed setting to enjoy a drink and take in the panoramic views. Duplex's combination of luxury, music, and spectacular views makes it a popular destination for both locals and tourists.

Another notable nightclub is Roxy, one of the oldest and most respected clubs in Prague. Situated in a former cinema in the Old Town, Roxy is known for its eclectic mix of electronic music, including techno, house, and drum and bass. The club regularly hosts both local and international DJs, as well as live performances. Roxy's industrial-style interior, with its exposed brick walls and open spaces, creates an edgy and energetic atmosphere. The club's commitment to showcasing innovative and cutting-edge music has cemented its reputation as a key player in Prague's nightlife scene.

For a more alternative and underground experience, Cross Club is a unique and eclectic venue that combines a nightclub, bar, and cultural space. Located in the Holešovice district, Cross Club is known for its distinctive decor, featuring recycled materials and intricate mechanical sculptures. The club's multi-level layout includes several dance floors and chill-out areas, each with its own unique design. Cross Club's music policy is diverse, ranging from electronic and techno to reggae and dubstep, and the venue regularly hosts live performances, DJ sets, and cultural events. The club's unconventional atmosphere and commitment to artistic expression make it a standout in Prague's nightlife scene.

Prague also offers a variety of live music venues that cater to different tastes and genres. One of the most renowned is Lucerna Music Bar, located near Wenceslas Square. This iconic venue has a rich history and has hosted numerous legendary artists over the years. Lucerna Music Bar features a diverse lineup of live performances, including rock, pop, and indie bands, as well as themed nights and dance parties. The venue's spacious interior, excellent acoustics, and lively atmosphere make it a favorite among music lovers.

Jazz enthusiasts will find plenty to enjoy in Prague, with several venues dedicated to this timeless genre. Reduta Jazz

Club, one of the oldest jazz clubs in Prague, has a storied history and has hosted performances by many renowned jazz musicians. The club's intimate setting, with its cozy seating and dim lighting, creates a perfect atmosphere for enjoying live jazz. Reduta's lineup includes a mix of local and international artists, performing everything from traditional jazz to contemporary fusion.

Another notable jazz venue is Jazz Dock, located on the banks of the Vltava River. This modern and stylish club offers stunning views of the river and the city, providing a unique backdrop for live performances. Jazz Dock features a diverse lineup of jazz, blues, and world music, with performances by both established and up-and-coming artists. The club's sleek design, excellent acoustics, and relaxed atmosphere make it a popular spot for both locals and visitors.

For those who prefer classical music, Prague is home to several prestigious concert halls that regularly host performances by world-class orchestras and soloists. The Rudolfinum, located on the banks of the Vltava River, is one of the most important cultural institutions in Prague. This neo-Renaissance building is home to the Czech Philharmonic Orchestra and features several beautiful concert halls, including the renowned Dvořák Hall. The Rudolfinum's rich history, stunning architecture, and exceptional acoustics make it a must-visit for classical music enthusiasts.

The Municipal House (Obecní dům) is another key venue for classical music in Prague. This stunning Art Nouveau building, located near the Powder Tower, is home to the Prague Symphony Orchestra and hosts a variety of concerts and cultural events. The building's beautiful Smetana Hall, with its intricate decor and excellent acoustics, provides a perfect setting for enjoying classical music. The Municipal House also features several other performance spaces, as well as a café and restaurant, making it a cultural hub in the heart of the city.

For a more intimate and unique experience, the Estates Theatre (Stavovské divadlo) offers a blend of history and music. This historic theatre, located in the Old Town, is one of the oldest opera houses in Europe and is renowned for its association with Wolfgang Amadeus Mozart, who conducted the premiere of his opera Don Giovanni here in 1787. The theatre regularly hosts performances of opera, ballet, and classical music, providing a rich cultural experience in a beautiful and historic setting.

Prague also has a thriving indie and alternative music scene, with several venues dedicated to showcasing up-and-coming artists and bands. MeetFactory, an arts center located in a former industrial building in the Smíchov district, is a key player in this scene. The venue hosts a diverse range of concerts, art exhibitions, and cultural events, providing a platform for experimental and alternative music. MeetFactory's raw and industrial setting, combined with its commitment to artistic innovation, makes it a unique and dynamic cultural space.

Another notable venue for alternative music is Palác Akropolis, located in the Žižkov district. This multi-functional space includes a concert hall, theatre, and bar, and hosts a wide range of performances, from indie and electronic music to theatre and dance. Palác Akropolis is known for its eclectic lineup and vibrant atmosphere, making it a popular spot for those looking to explore Prague's alternative music scene.

Unique Nightlife Experiences

Prague is a city that never sleeps, offering a plethora of unique nightlife experiences that go beyond the traditional bars and nightclubs. Whether you're looking to immerse yourself in the local culture, enjoy stunning views, or explore unconventional venues, Prague has something to offer for every type of night owl.

One of the most iconic and unique nightlife experiences in Prague is a visit to a traditional Czech beer garden. Letná Beer Garden, located in Letná Park, offers stunning views of the Vltava River and the city's skyline. This open-air venue is perfect for enjoying a cold beer on a warm evening while taking in the panoramic views of Prague. The casual and relaxed atmosphere, combined with the beauty of the surrounding park, makes it a popular spot for both locals and tourists. Another notable beer garden is Riegrovy Sady, situated in the Vinohrady district. This large, lively beer garden is known for its vibrant atmosphere and communal tables, making it an ideal place to meet new people and enjoy a refreshing drink.

For those looking to combine history with their nightlife experience, a visit to the Alchemist Bar is a must. Inspired by the mysterious world of alchemy, this bar offers a unique and immersive atmosphere, with its dim lighting, antique decor, and a menu of creatively crafted cocktails. The bar's signature drinks are served in unusual vessels and often come with theatrical presentations, adding to the overall experience. The Alchemist Bar's intriguing setting and innovative cocktails make it a standout in Prague's nightlife scene.

Another unique venue is the Anonymous Bar, which draws inspiration from the hacktivist group Anonymous. The bar's interior is filled with symbols and masks associated with the group, creating a mysterious and intriguing atmosphere. The cocktail menu is equally creative, featuring drinks that are served in unconventional ways, such as in light bulbs or test tubes. The Anonymous Bar's commitment to innovation and its distinctive theme make it a popular spot for those seeking a different kind of nightlife experience.

For a taste of the medieval, the Medieval Tavern (U krále Brabantského) offers a truly immersive experience. Located in a historic building in the Lesser Town, this tavern transports visitors back to the Middle Ages with its authentic decor, live entertainment, and hearty medieval fare. Guests can enjoy traditional dishes such as roasted meats, soups, and pies, all served by staff in period costumes. The highlight of the evening is the live entertainment, which includes fire shows, sword fighting, and belly dancing. The Medieval Tavern provides a unique and entertaining way to experience Prague's rich history and culture.

For those who enjoy live music, Jazz Dock is a must-visit. This modern and stylish jazz club is located on the banks of the Vltava River and offers stunning views of the water and the city. Jazz Dock features a diverse lineup of live performances, including jazz, blues, and world music, with both local and international artists taking the stage. The club's sleek design, excellent acoustics, and relaxed atmosphere make it a perfect spot to enjoy live music in an intimate setting.

Another unique nightlife experience is a visit to the Black Light Theatre. This form of theatre, which originated in Prague, uses black light and fluorescent costumes to create mesmerizing visual effects. The performances often combine dance, mime, and acrobatics, resulting in a captivating and otherworldly experience. One of the most famous black light theatres in Prague is the Image Theatre, which offers a variety of shows that are suitable for all ages. The innovative use of light and movement makes black light theatre a truly unique and unforgettable experience.

For a different kind of theatrical experience, the Prague Burlesque Show is a must-see. Held at the Royal Theatre, this glamorous and entertaining show features a mix of burlesque, cabaret, and circus acts. The performers, dressed in elaborate and dazzling costumes, deliver a high-energy and visually stunning performance that combines humor, sensuality, and artistry. The Prague Burlesque Show's blend of glamour and entertainment makes it a standout in the city's nightlife scene.

For those who enjoy exploring unconventional venues, the Bunkr Parukářka offers a unique and intriguing experience. This underground club is located in a former nuclear bunker in the Žižkov district and features a raw, industrial setting. The club hosts a variety of events, including live music, DJ sets, and art exhibitions, providing a platform for experimental and alternative culture. The Bunkr Parukářka's gritty and unconventional atmosphere, combined with its commitment to artistic expression, makes it a standout in Prague's nightlife landscape.

Another unconventional venue is the Cross Club, a multi-level space that combines a nightclub, bar, and cultural center. Located in the Holešovice district, Cross Club is known for its distinctive decor, featuring recycled materials and intricate mechanical sculptures. The club's music policy is diverse, ranging from electronic and techno to reggae and dubstep, and the venue regularly hosts live performances, DJ sets, and cultural events. The Cross Club's unique atmosphere and commitment to artistic innovation make it a must-visit for those seeking a different kind of nightlife experience.

For a more relaxed and intimate experience, a visit to one of Prague's rooftop bars is a great option. T-Anker, located on the roof of a shopping center in the Old Town, offers stunning views of the city, including Prague Castle and the Old Town Square. The bar's extensive beer selection, which includes both Czech and international brews, makes it a popular spot for beer enthusiasts. Another excellent rooftop bar is the Cloud 9 Sky Bar & Lounge, located on the top floor of the Hilton Prague. This stylish bar offers panoramic views of the city and a menu of creative cocktails and gourmet snacks. The combination of breathtaking views and sophisticated ambiance makes Cloud 9 a perfect spot for a romantic evening or a special night out.

For those interested in exploring Prague's nightlife further, several companies offer guided pub crawls that take visitors to some of the city's best bars and pubs. These tours provide an opportunity to sample a variety of drinks, meet new people, and experience Prague's nightlife in a fun and social setting. Whether you're interested in traditional Czech beer halls, modern cocktail bars, or unique and quirky spots, a pub crawl is a great way to discover the diverse and vibrant drinking scene in Prague.

CHAPTER 9

SHOPPING IN PRAGUE

Prague is not only a city of historical charm and architectural beauty but also a vibrant hub for shoppers seeking a diverse and enriching experience. The city offers a wide range of shopping opportunities, from luxury boutiques and modern shopping malls to traditional markets and unique local stores.

Start your shopping journey in Prague's historic center, where you will find a mix of high-end boutiques, international brands, and unique local shops. Parizska Street, located in the Old Town near the Old Town Square, is one of the most luxurious shopping streets in Prague. This elegant boulevard is lined with high-end boutiques from renowned international designers such as Louis Vuitton, Prada, Gucci, and Dior. The beautifully preserved Art Nouveau buildings add to the charm and sophistication of the shopping experience. Parizska Street is the perfect destination for those seeking luxury goods, designer fashion, and high-quality accessories.

Just a short walk from Parizska Street is Na Prikope, another popular shopping destination. This bustling avenue is home to a variety of international brands, including Zara, H&M, and Mango, as well as local Czech stores. Na Prikope is also known for its department stores, such as Debenhams and

Van Graaf, which offer a wide range of clothing, cosmetics, and accessories. The vibrant atmosphere and diverse selection of shops make Na Prikope a favorite among both locals and tourists.

For those looking to explore modern shopping malls, Palladium is a must-visit. Located in the heart of Prague near Republic Square, Palladium is the largest shopping center in the city, boasting over 200 shops, restaurants, and cafes. The mall offers a mix of international and local brands, ranging from fashion and electronics to beauty and home goods. The stylish and contemporary design of Palladium, combined with its extensive selection of stores, provides a comprehensive shopping experience in a convenient location.

Another notable shopping mall is Novy Smichov, located in the Smichov district. This modern shopping center features a wide range of stores, including popular international brands such as Marks & Spencer, Sephora, and Nike. Novy Smichov also offers a variety of dining options, a cinema, and a large supermarket, making it a one-stop destination for all your shopping needs. The mall's spacious layout and diverse selection of shops ensure a pleasant and enjoyable shopping experience.

For a more traditional shopping experience, head to Wenceslas Square, one of the main squares in Prague. This vibrant area is not only a cultural and historical hub but also a bustling shopping district. Wenceslas Square is home to a mix of department stores, boutiques, and souvenir shops, offering a wide range of products, from clothing and accessories to traditional Czech crafts. The square's central location and lively atmosphere make it a popular destination for both shopping and sightseeing.

Prague is also known for its unique and eclectic local stores, where you can find one-of-a-kind items and support local artisans. Manufaktura is a popular Czech brand that offers a range of handmade products, including natural cosmetics, wooden toys, and traditional crafts. The store's commitment to quality and sustainability makes it a great place to find unique and authentic Czech souvenirs. Manufaktura has several locations throughout Prague, including one near the Old Town Square.

For those interested in Czech glass and crystal, a visit to Moser is a must. This prestigious glassworks company, founded in 1857, is renowned for its high-quality, handcrafted crystal products. Moser's flagship store, located near the Old Town Square, offers a stunning selection of glassware, vases, and decorative items. The exquisite craftsmanship and timeless designs of Moser products make them a perfect souvenir or gift.

If you're a book lover, the Big Ben Bookshop is a hidden gem in Prague. Located in the Mala Strana district, this charming English-language bookstore offers a wide selection of books, including literature, travel guides, and children's books. The cozy and welcoming atmosphere of the Big Ben Bookshop makes it a perfect spot to browse for a new read or enjoy a quiet moment in the heart of the city.

For a truly unique shopping experience, visit one of Prague's traditional markets. Havelska Market, located in the Old Town, is one of the oldest markets in Prague, dating back to the 13th century. The market offers a variety of goods, including fresh produce, flowers, and handmade crafts. The lively atmosphere and colorful stalls make Havelska Market a delightful place to explore and find unique souvenirs.

Another notable market is the Naplavka Farmers Market, held every Saturday along the banks of the Vltava River. This popular market features a wide range of fresh, locally sourced produce, including fruits, vegetables, meats, and cheeses. In addition to food, the market also offers handmade crafts, flowers, and other artisanal products. The Naplavka Farmers Market is a great place to experience the local culture and enjoy the vibrant community atmosphere.

Prague also offers a variety of vintage and second-hand shops for those looking to discover unique and affordable finds. Boho Vintage Concept Store, located in the Vinohrady district, is a popular vintage shop that offers a carefully curated selection of clothing, accessories, and home decor items. The store's eclectic and stylish collection makes it a favorite among fashion enthusiasts and bargain hunters.

For those interested in antiques and collectibles, a visit to the Antikvariat Dlážděná is a must. This charming antique shop, located near Wenceslas Square, offers a wide range of items, including vintage books, maps, and prints. The shop's knowledgeable staff and extensive collection make it a great place to find unique and historically significant treasures.

CHAPTER 10

PRACTICAL INFORMATION

Money Matters

Understanding money matters is crucial for any visitor to Prague. This includes information on the local currency, exchange rates, banking services, payment methods, tipping customs, and budgeting tips.

The currency used in Prague and throughout the Czech Republic is the Czech koruna (CZK), also known as the crown. The koruna is divided into 100 haléřů, although coins in haléře are no longer in circulation. The currency comes in the following denominations: banknotes of 100, 200, 500, 1,000, 2,000, and 5,000 korunas, and coins of 1, 2, 5, 10, 20, and 50 korunas. Familiarizing yourself with the look and feel of the banknotes and coins can help you handle transactions more smoothly.

When it comes to exchanging money, it is advisable to avoid exchanging currency at airports or hotels, as they often offer less favorable exchange rates. Instead, look for reputable exchange offices in the city center, but always check the exchange rate and any fees before making a transaction. Some exchange offices advertise "no commission" but may offer a less favorable rate. It is wise to compare rates at different locations to get the best deal. For transparency, check the rate on the official Czech National Bank website or a reliable currency converter app.

Using ATMs is a convenient way to access cash in Prague. ATMs are widely available throughout the city, especially in tourist areas, shopping centers, and near major attractions. When using an ATM, ensure that it belongs to a reputable bank to avoid high withdrawal fees. Most ATMs offer instructions in multiple languages, including English. It is also important to inform your bank of your travel plans to avoid any issues with card usage. Be aware of any international withdrawal fees your bank may charge, and consider withdrawing larger amounts to minimize these fees.

Credit and debit cards are widely accepted in Prague, especially in hotels, restaurants, and larger shops. Visa and MasterCard are the most commonly accepted cards, while American Express and Diners Club may not be as widely accepted. However, it is always a good idea to carry some cash, particularly when visiting smaller establishments, markets, or when using public transportation, as some places may not accept cards. Contactless payments, including mobile payment options like Apple Pay and Google Pay, are also becoming increasingly popular in Prague.

Tipping customs in Prague are similar to those in many other European countries. In restaurants, it is customary to leave a tip of around 10% to 15% of the total bill if the service was satisfactory. Some restaurants may include a service charge in the bill, so it is important to check before adding an additional tip. When paying by card, it is common to leave the tip in cash. For other services, such as taxi rides, rounding up the fare or adding a small tip of about 10% is appreciated. In hotels, tipping the porter around 20 to 50 CZK per bag and leaving a small tip for housekeeping staff is also customary.

Budgeting for your trip to Prague depends on your travel style and preferences. Prague is known for being a relatively affordable destination compared to other major European cities. However, prices can vary significantly depending on where you eat, stay, and what activities you choose to do. For budget travelers, staying in hostels, eating at local eateries, and using public transportation can help keep costs low. Mid-range travelers can expect to spend more on hotels, dining at mid-range restaurants, and participating in guided tours or cultural activities. Luxury travelers can enjoy high-end accommodations, fine dining, and private tours, which will naturally come with a higher price tag.

Accommodation costs in Prague can vary widely. Budget options, such as hostels and budget hotels, can range from 300 to 1,200 CZK per night. Mid-range hotels and guesthouses typically cost between 1,200 and 3,000 CZK per night, while luxury hotels and boutique accommodations can range from 3,000 to 10,000 CZK or more per night. Booking in advance, especially during peak tourist seasons, can help secure better rates.

Food and dining expenses also vary depending on where and what you choose to eat. A meal at an inexpensive restaurant can cost around 150 to 300 CZK, while a three-course meal at a mid-range restaurant might cost between 500 and 1,000 CZK per person. Fine dining establishments can charge 1,000 CZK or more per person. Street food and local markets offer affordable and delicious options, with prices typically ranging from 50 to 200 CZK for snacks and small meals.

Transportation in Prague is efficient and affordable. A single ticket for public transportation, valid for 30 minutes, costs 30 CZK, while a 90-minute ticket costs 40 CZK. Day passes and multi-day passes are also available, offering unlimited travel on public transportation for the duration of the pass. Taxis are generally more expensive, with base fares starting around 40 CZK and additional charges per kilometer. Ride-sharing services like Uber and Bolt are also available and can be a more cost-effective option than traditional taxis.

Sightseeing and activities in Prague can range from free to quite expensive, depending on your interests. Many of Prague's iconic attractions, such as Charles Bridge, Old Town Square, and the Astronomical Clock, can be enjoyed for free. Entry fees for museums, galleries, and historical sites typically range from 100 to 350 CZK. Guided tours, river cruises, and cultural performances, such as opera or ballet, can cost anywhere from 500 to 2,000 CZK or more.

Shopping in Prague offers a variety of options, from luxury boutiques and international brands to local markets and souvenir shops. Prices for goods can vary, but haggling is generally not common practice in Prague. It is important to be aware of your budget and compare prices before making purchases, especially for high-value items such as Czech glass and crystal.

Staying Connected

Staying connected while traveling in Prague is essential for navigating the city, staying in touch with friends and family, accessing important information, and sharing your experiences in real-time.

When traveling to Prague, one of the first things you might want to do is obtain a local SIM card. This is often the most cost-effective way to stay connected, as it allows you to use local rates for calls, texts, and data. Major mobile network providers in the Czech Republic include T-Mobile, O2, and Vodafone. These providers offer a variety of prepaid SIM cards that cater to different needs and budgets. You can purchase a SIM card at airports, mobile phone shops, convenience stores, or directly from the providers' retail outlets. Activation is usually straightforward, requiring you to insert the SIM card into your phone and follow the instructions provided. It's important to ensure that your phone is unlocked and compatible with European networks before purchasing a local SIM card.

Prepaid SIM cards typically come with a certain amount of credit that can be used for calls, texts, and data. You can top up your credit at numerous locations, including convenience stores, supermarkets, and kiosks, or online through the provider's website. Data plans are usually available in various sizes, from small daily packages to larger monthly packages, allowing you to choose one that best suits your needs. Using a local SIM card can help you avoid expensive roaming charges and provide reliable internet access throughout your stay in Prague.

If you prefer not to switch SIM cards, consider using an international roaming plan from your home mobile provider. Many providers offer affordable roaming packages that include a set amount of data, calls, and texts that can be used in the Czech Republic. This option is convenient as it allows you to keep your existing phone number and contacts. However, it is important to check the costs and terms of your provider's roaming packages to ensure they are suitable for your usage needs.

Wi-Fi is widely available in Prague, making it easy to stay connected without relying solely on mobile data. Most hotels, hostels, and vacation rentals offer free Wi-Fi for guests, with the login details provided at check-in. Public

Wi-Fi hotspots are also common in cafes, restaurants, shopping centers, and tourist attractions. Some of the most popular cafes and chains, such as Starbucks and Costa Coffee, provide free Wi-Fi for customers. Libraries and public spaces often offer free Wi-Fi as well, making it easy to find a connection while exploring the city.

For those who need consistent and reliable internet access on the go, portable Wi-Fi devices are a great option. These devices, also known as mobile hotspots, allow you to create your own personal Wi-Fi network wherever you are. You can rent a portable Wi-Fi device from various providers, either before your trip or upon arrival in Prague. The rental process typically involves selecting a data plan, paying a rental fee, and picking up the device at the airport or having it delivered to your accommodation. Portable Wi-Fi devices are particularly useful for groups or families, as they allow multiple devices to connect to the internet simultaneously.

Using communication apps can help you stay in touch with friends and family without incurring high international call and text charges. Apps such as WhatsApp, Viber, Skype, and Facebook Messenger allow you to make voice and video calls, send text messages, and share photos and videos over the internet. These apps are free to download and use, provided you have an internet connection. Many of these apps also offer group chat and call features, making it easy to stay connected with multiple people at once.

For those who need to access work emails and files, cloud storage services such as Google Drive, Dropbox, and OneDrive are invaluable. These services allow you to store documents, photos, and other files online, making them accessible from any device with an internet connection. By uploading important files to the cloud before your trip, you can ensure that you have access to all necessary documents while in Prague. Additionally, many cloud storage services offer collaboration features, enabling you to share files and work on documents with others in real-time.

If you need to make local calls while in Prague, consider using a VoIP (Voice over Internet Protocol) service such as Skype or Google Voice. These services allow you to make phone calls over the internet, often at much lower rates than traditional phone calls. You can use these services to call local numbers, as well as international numbers, making them a versatile option for staying connected.

Staying informed about local news and events is also important while traveling. Many news websites and apps offer English-language versions, allowing you to stay updated on the latest happenings in Prague and the Czech Republic. Some popular English-language news sources include Prague Daily Monitor, Prague TV, and Radio Prague International. These sources provide news, weather updates, and information on local events, helping you stay informed and make the most of your time in Prague.

Using navigation apps can help you get around the city with ease. Google Maps and Apple Maps are both excellent options for finding your way around Prague. These apps provide detailed maps, directions, and public transportation information, making it easy to navigate the city. You can also download offline maps before your trip, ensuring you have access to navigation even without an internet connection. Other useful apps include Citymapper, which offers detailed public transportation information, and Uber or Bolt, which can be used to book rides within the city.

For language assistance, translation apps such as Google Translate can be incredibly helpful. Google Translate offers translations between multiple languages, including Czech and English. The app also features a conversation mode, which allows you to have real-time translated conversations with others. Additionally, the camera translation feature can be used to translate text in images, such as signs or menus, making it easier to navigate and communicate in Prague.

Medical and Emergency Services

Understanding medical and emergency services in Prague is essential for any traveler, ensuring peace of mind and preparedness in case of health issues or emergencies.

Prague, as the capital city of the Czech Republic, boasts a well-developed healthcare system that provides a range of medical services. The city is home to numerous hospitals, clinics, and specialized medical centers, offering high-quality care to both residents and visitors. The healthcare system in the Czech Republic is a mix of public and private providers, with public healthcare being accessible to all citizens and residents through a system funded by health insurance contributions.

In case of a medical emergency, knowing the emergency numbers and how to access emergency services is crucial. The universal emergency number in the Czech Republic is 112, which can be dialed for free from any phone, including mobile phones without a SIM card. This number connects callers to the emergency services dispatcher, who can send an ambulance, fire brigade, or police, depending on the nature of the emergency. Additionally, specific emergency numbers include 155 for medical emergencies, 150 for the fire brigade, and 158 for the police. It is advisable to save these numbers in your phone and have them readily accessible during your stay in Prague.

If you require immediate medical attention, Prague has several hospitals with emergency departments that are well-equipped to handle various medical emergencies. Some of the major hospitals include the General University Hospital (Všeobecná fakultní nemocnice) located near Charles Square, which is one of the largest and most comprehensive medical facilities in the city. Another notable hospital is the Motol University Hospital (Fakultní nemocnice v Motole), which is known for its specialized care and has a dedicated children's hospital as well. These hospitals have emergency departments that operate 24/7 and are staffed by experienced medical professionals who can provide urgent care.

In addition to hospitals, Prague has numerous clinics and medical centers that offer a wide range of healthcare services. These include general practitioners, specialists, dental clinics, and physiotherapy centers. Many clinics cater specifically to expatriates and tourists, with English-speaking staff and a focus on providing accessible and efficient care. One such clinic is the Canadian Medical Care, which offers a comprehensive range of medical services, including general practice, pediatrics, gynecology, and dental care. The clinic has multiple locations throughout Prague and provides services in multiple languages, including English, German, and Russian.

For non-emergency medical issues, it is often best to visit a general practitioner (GP) or a local clinic. General practitioners can diagnose and treat a wide range of common illnesses and conditions, and they can refer patients to specialists if needed. It is advisable to make an appointment in advance, although some clinics also offer walk-in services for urgent but non-emergency situations. When visiting a GP or clinic, it is important to bring your identification and any relevant medical documents or health insurance information.

Pharmacies (lékarna) are widely available throughout Prague and provide an essential service for obtaining prescription medications, over-the-counter drugs, and health-related products. Many pharmacies in Prague have extended hours, and some operate 24/7. In case you need medication outside regular business hours, there are several late-night pharmacies located in the city center, such as the Benu Pharmacy at Wenceslas Square. Pharmacists in Prague are well-trained and can offer advice on minor health issues, recommend over-the-counter treatments, and fill prescriptions from doctors.

Health insurance is an important consideration for travelers to Prague. The Czech Republic has agreements with several countries, including those in the European Union, that allow for reciprocal healthcare coverage. Travelers from EU countries should bring their European Health Insurance Card (EHIC), which provides access to medically necessary public healthcare services at the same cost as residents. For travelers from non-EU countries, it is advisable to have comprehensive travel insurance that includes health coverage. Travel insurance can help cover the cost of medical treatment, emergency evacuation, and other health-related expenses that may arise during your trip.

If you require specialized medical care, Prague has several hospitals and clinics that offer a range of specialized services. These include cardiology, oncology, orthopedics, neurology, and more. The Institute of Clinical and Experimental Medicine (IKEM) is one of the leading specialized hospitals in Prague, known for its advanced treatments in cardiology, transplantology, and diabetes care. Another notable institution is the Na Homolce Hospital, which specializes in neurosurgery, cardiology, and oncology. These specialized centers are equipped with state-of-the-art technology and staffed by highly qualified medical professionals.

In the event of a dental emergency, Prague has numerous dental clinics that provide both routine and emergency dental care. It is advisable to contact a dental clinic directly to schedule an appointment or seek emergency treatment. Many dental clinics in Prague offer services in multiple languages and can accommodate tourists and expatriates. Some well-regarded dental clinics include the Prague Dental Clinic and the Dental Clinic Jan Stuchlík, both of which offer a range of dental services, including preventive care, restorative treatments, and emergency dental procedures.

For those requiring mental health support, Prague offers a range of mental health services, including counseling, psychotherapy, and psychiatric care. There are several clinics and private practitioners who provide mental health services in multiple languages, making it accessible for expatriates and tourists. The Prague Integration Psychotherapy Clinic is one such facility that offers counseling and therapy in English, focusing on the mental health needs of the international community in Prague.

Practical tips for accessing medical care in Prague include keeping a list of important contact numbers, carrying a basic first aid kit, and knowing the location of the nearest medical facilities. It is also helpful to have a basic understanding of Czech medical terminology, although many medical professionals in Prague speak English. In case of a medical emergency, it is important to remain calm and provide clear information to emergency responders, including your location and the nature of the emergency.

Avoiding Tourist Traps

Prague is a beautiful and historic city that attracts millions of tourists each year. However, like many popular destinations, it also has its fair share of tourist traps. These are places or experiences that are designed to extract money from visitors without offering much in return.

One of the most common tourist traps in Prague is overpriced restaurants and cafes, especially those located near major tourist attractions like the Old Town Square, Charles Bridge, and Wenceslas Square. These establishments often charge significantly higher prices for food and drinks compared to places just a short walk away. To avoid this, it is advisable to venture a bit further from the main tourist areas and explore local neighborhoods such as Vinohrady, Žižkov, or Holešovice, where you can find excellent restaurants and cafes at more reasonable prices. Look for places that are frequented by locals rather than those that heavily advertise in multiple languages or have menu boards with pictures.

Another common trap is currency exchange offices that offer poor exchange rates or charge high fees. These are often located in tourist-heavy areas and advertise "no commission" to lure in unsuspecting visitors. However, the exchange rates they offer are usually much worse than the official rate. To get the best rates, use ATMs from reputable banks, or visit exchange offices that display the official exchange rate and clearly state any fees. It's also a good idea to check the exchange rate online before changing money so you have a clear idea of what to expect.

Taxis can also be a source of frustration for tourists in Prague, as some drivers may overcharge or take longer routes to increase the fare. To avoid this, it is best to use reputable taxi companies such as AAA Radiotaxi or City Taxi. You can also use ride-sharing services like Uber or Bolt, which offer transparent pricing and the ability to track your route in real-time. If you must take a traditional taxi, ensure the meter is running and agree on an approximate fare before starting the journey.

Another area where tourists can easily be taken advantage of is in souvenir shopping. Many shops in tourist areas sell generic, mass-produced items at inflated prices, often marketed as authentic Czech products. To find genuine and unique souvenirs, consider visiting local markets, craft shops, or stores that specialize in traditional Czech goods. For example, Manufaktura offers high-quality, locally made products, including cosmetics, wooden toys, and traditional crafts. Additionally, look for shops that carry Bohemian glass or garnet jewelry, both of which are traditional Czech products.

Tour guides and tours can also be a hit-or-miss experience. While many offer valuable insights and a rich historical context, some may provide limited information and focus more on getting you to spend money at affiliated shops or restaurants. To ensure you get a quality experience, consider using well-reviewed tour companies or guides recommended by trusted sources. Alternatively, you can explore the city on your own using guidebooks or self-guided tour apps that provide detailed information and the freedom to explore at your own pace.

Attractions and activities that appear too good to be true often are. For example, boat tours along the Vltava River can be a delightful experience, but some operators charge high prices for short trips with limited views. To avoid this, research and book with reputable companies that offer good value for money. Similarly, be cautious of offers for concert tickets, especially those sold on the street. These may be overpriced or for performances of lower quality. Instead, purchase tickets directly from venues or through official ticketing websites.

Another way to avoid tourist traps is to be cautious of street performers and beggars in popular tourist areas. While some performers are talented and provide genuine entertainment, others may aggressively solicit money or operate in groups to distract and pickpocket tourists. It's wise to enjoy street performances from a distance and keep an eye on your belongings. When approached by beggars, it's best to politely decline and continue on your way, as some may be part of organized groups that target tourists.

Overpriced and low-quality food stands are another common sight in tourist-heavy areas. While it can be tempting to grab a quick bite from a street vendor, these stalls often sell mediocre food at inflated prices. Instead, look for food stalls that are popular with locals, as they are more likely to offer authentic and reasonably priced snacks. Visiting local markets such as the Naplavka Farmers Market can also provide a more authentic and enjoyable food experience.

Tours and activities that promise exclusive access or VIP experiences should be approached with caution. While some may offer genuine value, others may be overpriced and fail to deliver on their promises. Always research and read reviews before booking such experiences to ensure they are worth the cost.

In addition to these specific tips, it's important to approach your trip to Prague with a general sense of awareness and skepticism. If something seems too good to be true or if you feel pressured into making a purchase or booking, it's often best to walk away and take some time to research your options. Trust your instincts and don't be afraid to ask questions or seek advice from locals or fellow travelers.

Finally, one of the best ways to avoid tourist traps is to plan your trip carefully and do your research. By familiarizing yourself with the city, its culture, and the common scams and traps, you can navigate Prague more confidently and make the most of your visit. Use trusted travel resources, seek recommendations from friends or online communities, and be open to exploring off-the-beaten-path destinations that offer a more authentic and rewarding experience.

Cultural Etiquette

Understanding and respecting cultural etiquette in Prague is essential for making the most of your visit and ensuring a positive experience with the local people. By familiarizing yourself with these aspects of Czech culture, you can interact more comfortably and respectfully with locals, enriching your travel experience.

When meeting someone for the first time, it is customary to shake hands and make direct eye contact. This applies to both men and women. A firm handshake is considered polite, and maintaining eye contact shows sincerity and interest. When greeting friends or close acquaintances, a light kiss on each cheek or a hug may be appropriate, but this is less common with new acquaintances.

In formal situations, it is respectful to use titles and last names until you are invited to use first names. For example, address men as "pan" followed by their last name, and women as "paní" (married) or "slečna" (unmarried) followed by their last name. Using first names without being invited to do so can be considered overly familiar or disrespectful.

Czechs value politeness and quietness in public spaces. Loud conversations, excessive noise, or disruptive behavior are generally frowned upon. When using public transportation, it is customary to offer your seat to the elderly, pregnant women, and those with disabilities. It is also important to stand on the right side of escalators to allow others to pass on the left.

When dining in a restaurant, wait to be seated by the host or server. It is customary to greet the staff with "dobrý den" (good day) upon entering. Once seated, it is polite to keep your hands visible and resting on the table, but not your elbows. When the meal arrives, wait for everyone to be served before starting to eat. If you are the guest, it is polite to wait for the host to start eating first.

Czechs typically use utensils for most foods, including pizza and sandwiches. When finished with your meal, place your knife and fork parallel on the plate to signal that you are done. Tipping is appreciated but not obligatory. A tip of around 10% of the total bill is customary if the service was satisfactory. It is common to round up the bill rather than leaving coins.

If you are invited to someone's home, it is customary to bring a small gift as a token of appreciation. Suitable gifts include flowers (but avoid giving an even number of flowers as it is associated with funerals), chocolates, wine, or a small souvenir from your home country. When giving flowers, remove the wrapping before presenting them. It is also polite to offer to remove your shoes upon entering a home, and many hosts will provide slippers for guests.

Czechs tend to dress conservatively, especially in professional and formal settings. Business attire typically includes suits and ties for men, and dresses or suits for women. In more casual settings, such as visiting friends or going to a local pub, smart-casual attire is appropriate. It is important to dress modestly when visiting religious sites, covering shoulders and knees as a sign of respect.

Czechs value direct and honest communication. They appreciate straightforwardness and clarity in conversations. However, it is important to be tactful and avoid being overly blunt or confrontational. Humility and modesty are valued traits, so boasting or showing off is generally frowned upon. In professional settings, it is common to engage in small talk before getting down to business, but this is usually brief.

Punctuality is highly valued in Czech culture. Whether you have a business meeting, social gathering, or appointment, it is important to arrive on time. Being late is considered disrespectful and unprofessional. If you are running late, it is courteous to inform the person you are meeting as soon as possible.

Czechs celebrate a variety of cultural and religious holidays throughout the year. These include Christmas, Easter, and national holidays such as Czech Independence Day on October 28th. During these times, many businesses may be closed, and public events and celebrations may take place. It is important to respect these traditions and participate in a respectful and appreciative manner.

When visiting religious sites, such as churches or synagogues, it is important to show respect by dressing modestly and behaving quietly. It is customary to remove your hat and avoid using flash photography. Observing and participating in local customs, such as Christmas markets or Easter egg decorating, can enhance your cultural experience and show your appreciation for Czech traditions.

Czech culture has been shaped by its complex history, including periods of occupation and political change. It is important to be aware of this historical context when engaging in conversations with locals. Topics such as World War II, communism, and the Velvet Revolution can be sensitive subjects. Approach these topics with respect and an open mind, and avoid making assumptions or uninformed statements.

Czechs take pride in their natural environment and have a strong emphasis on environmental conservation. It is important to follow local practices for recycling and waste disposal. When visiting parks and natural areas, respect the environment by staying on designated paths, not littering, and respecting wildlife. Participating in eco-friendly practices, such as using public transportation or cycling, can also show your respect for the local environment.

Czechs are known for their hospitality and friendliness, but they can also be reserved with strangers. Building trust and rapport may take time, but once established, friendships with Czechs can be very rewarding. Showing genuine interest in Czech culture, language, and traditions can help build positive relationships. Learning a few basic phrases in Czech, such as "please" (prosím), "thank you" (děkuji), and "excuse me" (promiňte), can go a long way in showing respect and appreciation for the local culture.

While it is common to take photos and share experiences on social media, it is important to be mindful of privacy and cultural sensitivity. Always ask for permission before taking photos of people, especially in private or sensitive settings. Avoid posting images that could be considered disrespectful or intrusive. When sharing your experiences online, be respectful and considerate of how your posts may be perceived by others.

CHAPTER 11

DAY TRIPS FROM PRAGUE

Day trips from Prague offer a wonderful way to explore the rich history, stunning landscapes, and charming towns of the Czech Republic. There are numerous destinations within a short distance from the capital that provide a variety of experiences, from medieval castles and spa towns to natural parks and historical sites.

One of the most popular day trips from Prague is to the town of Český Krumlov. Located about 170 kilometers south of Prague, this UNESCO World Heritage site is renowned for its well-preserved medieval architecture, winding streets, and picturesque setting along the Vltava River. The centerpiece of Český Krumlov is its stunning castle, which dates back to the 13th century. Visitors can explore the castle's beautifully decorated interiors, expansive gardens, and the iconic Castle Tower, which offers breathtaking views of the town and surrounding countryside. The town also boasts several museums, galleries, and charming cafes, making it a delightful destination for a day trip.

Another must-visit destination is the town of Kutná Hora, located approximately 80 kilometers east of Prague. Kutná Hora is famous for its historical significance as a major silver mining center in the medieval period. The town's wealth and prominence are reflected in its stunning architecture, particularly the Gothic masterpiece of St. Barbara's Church. This impressive cathedral is adorned with intricate frescoes, stained glass windows, and a unique vaulted ceiling. Another highlight of Kutná Hora is the Sedlec Ossuary, also known as the Bone Church. This small chapel is decorated with the bones of over 40,000 people, arranged in macabre and fascinating patterns. The town also offers several other historical sites, such as the Italian Court, which once served as the royal mint, and the Hrádek museum, which provides insight into the town's mining history.

A visit to the spa town of Karlovy Vary is another excellent day trip option. Located about 130 kilometers west of Prague, Karlovy Vary is renowned for its hot springs and elegant architecture. The town has been a popular spa destination since the 19th century, attracting visitors from all over the world. The town's colonnades, such as the Mill Colonnade and the Market Colonnade, are home to numerous mineral springs where visitors can sample the healing waters. In addition to its spa facilities, Karlovy Vary is known for its beautiful Art Nouveau and Baroque buildings, scenic parks, and the iconic Grandhotel Pupp. The town also hosts the annual Karlovy Vary International Film Festival, one of the oldest and most prestigious film festivals in Europe.

For those interested in exploring the natural beauty of the Czech Republic, a day trip to the Bohemian Switzerland National Park is highly recommended. Located about 120 kilometers north of Prague, this national park is famous for its dramatic sandstone formations, deep gorges, and lush forests. One of the park's most iconic landmarks is the Pravčická Brána, the largest natural sandstone arch in Europe. Visitors can hike to this stunning rock formation and enjoy panoramic views of the surrounding landscape. The park also offers a variety of hiking and biking trails, scenic viewpoints, and the opportunity to take a boat ride through the picturesque Kamenice River Gorge.

The town of Terezín, located about 60 kilometers north of Prague, offers a sobering and educational day trip experience. Terezín was originally built as a military fortress in the late 18th century but is best known for its role during World War II as a Nazi concentration camp and ghetto. Visitors can explore the Terezín Memorial, which includes the Small Fortress, the Ghetto Museum, and the National Cemetery. These sites provide a poignant and informative look at the history of the Holocaust and the experiences of those who were imprisoned at Terezín. The town also features several historical buildings and monuments, offering a deeper understanding of this dark period in history.

For a taste of medieval history and stunning architecture, a visit to the town of Karlštejn is a must. Located about 30 kilometers southwest of Prague, Karlštejn is home to the magnificent Karlštejn Castle. This Gothic castle was founded in the 14th century by Emperor Charles IV and served as a royal treasury and a place to safeguard the crown jewels and holy relics. Visitors can take guided tours of the castle's various chambers, including the impressive Chapel of the Holy Cross, which is adorned with semi-precious stones and gold. The town itself is charming, with quaint streets, local shops, and restaurants offering traditional Czech cuisine.

Another fascinating day trip destination is the town of Pilsen, located about 90 kilometers west of Prague. Pilsen is best known as the birthplace of Pilsner beer, and a visit to the Pilsner Urquell Brewery is a highlight for many visitors. The brewery offers guided tours that provide insight into the brewing process, the history of Pilsner beer, and the opportunity to sample fresh beer straight from the barrel. In addition to its brewing heritage, Pilsen boasts several historical and cultural attractions, including the Gothic St. Bartholomew's Cathedral, the Great Synagogue, and the Pilsen Historical Underground, a network of tunnels and cellars dating back to the 14th century.

For those interested in exploring the royal history of the Czech Republic, a visit to the town of Konopiště is highly recommended. Located about 50 kilometers southeast of Prague, Konopiště is home to the stunning Konopiště Castle, which was the residence of Archduke Franz Ferdinand of Austria, whose assassination in 1914 triggered the start of World War I. The castle is beautifully preserved and features lavish interiors, extensive collections of art and hunting trophies, and well-manicured gardens. Visitors can take guided tours of the castle and learn about its history and the life of its most famous resident.

CONCLUSION

As your journey through Prague and its surroundings comes to an end, it is clear that this city, with its rich history, stunning architecture, vibrant culture, and welcoming atmosphere, offers an unparalleled travel experience. From the iconic landmarks and hidden gems within Prague to the enchanting day trips that take you deeper into the Czech countryside, every corner of this region holds a story waiting to be discovered.

Prague is a city that captivates the senses and leaves an indelible mark on the heart. Its cobblestone streets echo with the footsteps of history, and its breathtaking views inspire awe and wonder. The majestic Prague Castle, the timeless beauty of Charles Bridge, the bustling energy of Old Town Square, and the serene expanses of Letná Park all contribute to the city's unique charm. The blend of Gothic, Baroque, Renaissance, and modern architecture paints a vivid picture of Prague's past and present, showcasing its evolution through the centuries.

Exploring the neighborhoods of Prague reveals a tapestry of experiences, from the artistic vibes of Vinohrady and the alternative spirit of Žižkov to the historic elegance of Malá Strana and the modern pulse of New Town. Each area offers its own distinct character and hidden treasures, inviting you to delve deeper and uncover the essence of the city.

Beyond Prague, the Czech Republic unfolds a diverse landscape of cultural and natural wonders. The medieval charm of Český Krumlov, the spa heritage of Karlovy Vary, the historical significance of Kutná Hora, and the breathtaking scenery of Bohemian Switzerland National Park are just a few of the many destinations that enrich your travel experience. These day trips provide a deeper understanding of the country's rich heritage and natural beauty, offering a perfect complement to your time in Prague.

Throughout your travels, the warmth and hospitality of the Czech people add a personal touch to your journey. The cultural etiquette, local customs, and traditions that you have embraced along the way create meaningful connections and foster a sense of belonging. Whether you are enjoying a traditional meal in a family-owned restaurant, participating in a local festival, or simply engaging in a friendly conversation with a resident, these interactions enhance your understanding and appreciation of Czech culture.

As you prepare to leave this enchanting city, take with you the memories of its beauty, the taste of its cuisine, the melody of its music, and the stories of its people. Let these experiences inspire you to continue exploring the world with an open mind and a curious heart. Prague is not just a destination; it is a journey into history, art, and culture—a journey that stays with you long after you have left its cobblestone streets behind.

Made in the USA
Las Vegas, NV
06 January 2025

15960763R00115